PHalarope Books

PHalarope books are designed specifically for the amateur naturalist. These volumes represent excellence in natural history publishing. Each book in the PHalarope series is based on a nature course or program at the college or adult education level or is sponsored by a museum or nature center. Each PHalarope book reflects the author's teaching ability as well as writing ability. Among the books:

THOREAU'S METHOD

A Handbook for Nature Study

DAVID PEPI

A SPECTRUM BOOK

Prentice-Hall, Inc., Englewood Cliffs, New Jersey 07632

Library of Congress Cataloging in Publication Data

Pepi, David.
    Thoreau's method.

    (PHalarope books)
    "A Spectrum Book."
    Includes bibliographies and index.
    1. Nature study.   I. Title.
QH51.P39   1984   574'.0723   84-13326
ISBN   0-13-919887-3
ISBN   0-13-919879-2 (pbk.)

This book is available at a special discount when ordered
in bulk quantities. Contact Prentice-Hall, Inc., General
Publishing Division, Special Sales, Englewood Cliffs, N.J. 07632.

1 2 3 4 5 6 7 8 9 10

Editorial/production supervision by Chris McMorrow
Cover design by Hal Siegel
Illustrations by Eva Dorfman
Manufacturing buyer: Frank Grieco

ISBN 0-13-919887-3

ISBN 0-13-919879-2 {PBK.}

Prentice-Hall International, Inc., *London*
Prentice-Hall of Australia Pty. Limited, *Sydney*
Prentice-Hall Canada Inc., *Toronto*
Prentice-Hall of India Private Limited, *New Delhi*
Prentice-Hall of Japan, Inc., *Tokyo*
Prentice-Hall of Southeast Asia Pte. Ltd., *Singapore*
Whitehall Books Limited, *Wellington, New Zealand*
Editora Prentice-Hall do Brasil Ltda., *Rio de Janeiro*
Prentice-Hall Hispanoamericana, S.A., *Mexico*

To Professor Richard A. Baer, Jr., director of the
Program in Agricultural and Environmental Ethics
at Cornell University and connoisseur
of Cayuga Basin cantaloupes.

Contents

Preface

This is a how-to book on nature appreciation as it was done by Henry David Thoreau. In it you'll learn how to cup a wasp in your hands without getting stung, how to use a brandy snifter to enjoy wildflowers, and how to get the most out of the fall migration of broad-winged hawks. These, however, are only minor techniques, and if they were all you were to learn about appreciating nature, you'd be left with a mere bag of tricks that would soon lose its power to satisfy. Sustained satisfaction comes only when you understand enough about the overall process of appreciating to apply specific techniques methodologically. Therefore, the method of nature appreciation that Thoreau used is explained at the outset, and all subsequent activities are based on it.

The book is arranged sequentially. Thoreau's method—which consists of deliberately integrating thinking, feeling, and acting in order to obtain the richest experiences possible from natural objects and events—is explained in Chapter 1. Chapters 2 and 3 contain suggestions for choosing books, clothing, and equipment in keeping with this approach and the go-light philosophy that it entails. A natural system of navigation is described in the first part of Chapter 4, and in the second part directions are given for supplementing that system with basic map and compass skills. Chapter 5 is devoted to the art of walking, the principal technique used by nature appreciators. And finally, Chapters 6 through 10 contain directions for excursions that will enable you to put the material in the first five chapters to the test. Each of the excursions is for one day or less, and each involves plants and animals that are common in much of eastern North America (for example, underwing moths, goldenrods, tulip trees, pitcher plants, broad-winged hawks, and Canada geese).

Every chapter except the first ends with five thought questions and a list of recommended readings. The thought questions are *not* there to test your comprehension. Each is offered as a black walnut, something tasty to crack and tease at. In most instances, the hints that accompany the questions give the answers away, so if all you want is a little help, read just the first part of each hint. The recommended readings will lead you to many excellent books and articles on nature.

Definite opinions—on equipment from boots to binoculars and on techniques from sharpening jackknives to finding your way in the woods without a compass—appear throughout the book. Reasons are given for each opinion, but even so, you'll find occasions on which to disagree. That's as it should be. Nature appreciation as presented here is an intelligent activity open to inquiry and capable of being improved through reasoned discourse. Besides, when two outdoor enthusiasts agree completely on jackknives, boots, and walking sticks, at least one of them doesn't know what he or she is talking about.

The directions for the excursions in Chapters 6 through 10 have been field-tested. They work. That doesn't mean you'll see broad-winged hawks and black moths with 6-inch wingspreads every time you go out looking for them, but you can be sure that only the second half of Chapter 10 will lead you on a wild-goose chase.

Acknowledgments

Thanks to Jeanne W. Lawless, qualitative naturalist first class. Jeanne and I developed the idea of qualitative natural history, planned this book, and did many of the things described in it while walking in the Cayuga Basin together. Jeanne also did a great deal of the preliminary editing, so in many ways this book is hers.

Special thanks to Professor Richard A. Baer, Jr., for suggesting that the literature of wine connoisseurship might shed light on nature appreciation and for providing me with the financial support needed to complete this book; to Professor Verne N. Rockcastle for suggesting that this book be written and for putting me in touch with the publisher; and to Professor D. Bob Gowin for the theory of valuing on which this book is based and for the terms used in the first chapter.

I am also grateful to the following individuals: Dr. John Rawlins, for introducing me to mothing, including the use of phenyl acetaldehyde; Professor John G. Franclemont, for demonstrating the fine points of "running a sheet"; Professor Richard B. Fischer, for several of the techniques used in the chapters on goldenrods and bogs; Professor F. Ross, for his dissertation on goldenrod galls ("Solidago Cecidology," Cornell University, 1936); Professor L. D. Uhler, for his dissertation on the goldenrod gall fly ("The Biology and Ecology of the Goldenrod Gall Fly," Cornell University, 1948; see also _Biology and Ecology of the Goldenrod Gall Fly, Cornell University, Agricultural Experiment Station Memorandum Number 300_, 51 pp.). Other authorities from whom I have drawn heavily are mentioned in the text. No doubt, still others have been overlooked, and to these contributors go my apologies as well as my promise to make amends, if they will tell me how.

The following institutions were helpful to me and I thank them: the Department of Natural Resources at Cornell University, for a Postdoctoral Fellowship and access to a stimulating community of scientists and scholars; the Cornell University libraries—particularly the reference librarians and staff members at the Albert R. Mann Library, the John M. Olin Library, the Entomology Library, and the Uris Library—for expert and patient assistance; the Jessie

Smith Noyes Foundation, for financial support while writing; the Elm Research Institute, for a grant that supported research that led to this book; and the Andrew W. Mellon Foundation, for a similar grant.

Finally, thanks to Tom Demmo, a woodsman who knows the value of a hat that sheds the rain.

The second epigraph on page 3 is taken from John Muir's *The Yosemite* (New York: The Century Co., 1912), p. 28. It is reprinted by permission of E. P. Dutton, Inc.

Pages 14 and 36 contain quotes from "Nessmuk" (George W. Sears), *Woodcraft and Camping* (New York: Forest and Stream Publishing Co., 1920; reprint ed., New York: Dover Publications, Inc., 1963), p. 3. They are used by permission.

Page 41 contains a quote from "Two Tramps in Mud Time" from *The Poetry of Robert Frost*, edited by Edward Connery Lathem. Copyright 1936 by Robert Frost. Copyright © 1964 by Lesley Frost Ballantine. Copyright © 1969 by Holt, Rinehart and Winston. Reprinted by permission of Holt, Rinehart and Winston, Publishers, the Estate of Robert Frost, and Jonathan Cape Ltd., London.

The quote on page 41 from T. S. Eliot's "The Waste Land" is taken from *Collected Poems 1909–1962* by T. S. Eliot, copyright 1936 by Harcourt Brace Jovanovich, Inc.; copyright © 1963, 1964, by T. S. Eliot. Reprinted by permission of Harcourt Brace Jovanovich, Inc., and Faber and Faber Publishers, London.

The excerpt on page 42 from John Muir's *The Mountains of California* (New York: The Century Co., 1898), Chapter 10, "A Windstorm in the Forests," pp. 251–252, is reprinted by permission of E. P. Dutton, Inc.

The quote on page 57 and Figure 4.1's source are from *Nature is Your Guide* by Harold Gatty, copyright © 1958 by the Executors of the Estate of Harold Gatty. Reprinted by permission of E. P. Dutton, publisher, and A. Fenna Gatty.

Scattered quotations from Henry David Thoreau's writings were originally published by Houghton Mifflin Co., Boston, 1906.

Lawrence W. Swan's quote from "Goose of the Himalayas" on page 169 is used with permission from *Natural History*, Vol. 79, No. 8; copyright the American Museum of Natural History, 1970.

Figures 10.1 and 10.2 are loosely based on the illustrations that appear on pages 131, 132, and 133 of the following article: Cone, Clarence D. Jr., "The Soaring Flight of Birds," _Scientific American_, Volume 206, No. 4, April 1962, pp. 130–140. Copyright © 1962 by Scientific American, Inc. All rights reserved.

Figure 10.3 is based on "Formation Flight of Birds," Lissaman, P/B.S., _Science_, Vol. 168, pp. 1003–1005, Figure 1, May 22, 1970, Copyright © 1970 by the American Association for the Advancement of Science.

SKILLS

CHAPTER ONE
Making Nature Satisfy

It requires more than a day's devotion to know and to possess the wealth of a day.

Henry David Thoreau
"Life Without Principle"
Writings, Vol. 4, 1906

One must labor for beauty as for bread, here [the wilderness] as elsewhere.

John Muir
The Yosemite, 1912

Start at the top. If you want to get smart about appreciating nature, analyze Henry David Thoreau's "Wild Apples"; then go on to similar essays by other first-rate nature writers. You'll find that sophisticated nature appreciators work like virtuous wine connoisseurs. Of course, this similarity holds only if you don't confuse the wine connoisseur with the wine snob. A wine snob adopts arbitrary and often obscure standards and then uses them to pronounce particular wines good or bad. In contrast, a wine connoisseur deliberately combines knowledge and sensory techniques in order to obtain the richest experience possible from *any* wine, and then he or she publishes the results so as to make the satisfactions enjoyed available to all. Henry David Thoreau, John Burroughs, John Muir, Anna Botsford Comstock, and other literary naturalists were doing the same thing, but instead of wines, they were working with pines and hemlocks.

The approach Thoreau and the others used will be referred to as *qualitative natural history*, and it is explained below. The explanation is relatively abstract compared with the material in the remaining chapters, but it's important to rise above specifics at the outset in order to view the process of nature appreciation as a whole. This perspective and the understanding that comes with it will enable you to apply the material in the rest of the book methodologically. We'll begin by defining qualitative natural history; then we'll analyze the elements and relationships involved in a simple but ideal instance of it.

Qualitative Natural History

Qualitative natural history is a form of nature appreciation in which thinking, feeling, and acting are integrated deliberately in order to obtain the richest experiences possible from natural objects and occurrences.

APPRECIATING THE SWEET VIBURNUM

An instance of qualitative natural history always involves relationships among four major elements: (1) an *event*, a person experiencing a natural object or occurrence, (2) *meanings*, knowledge concerning the event, (3) *feelings*, emotions and sensations that attend the event, and (4) *felt-significance*, a culminating sense of warranted satisfaction (terms drawn from *Educating* by D. Bob Gowin; see Recommended Reading). An example will help illustrate the meanings of these terms.

A hiker walking along a woodland path in springtime gradually becomes aware of feeling pleased and attracted. With thought, the object of these sensations is found to be a fragrance. After looking and sniffing about, a connection is made between the fragrance and the white flowers on a tall shrub. The hiker uses a field guide to identify the shrub as a benign plant called sweet viburnum (*Viburnum lentago*). At home, other books are used to find out as much about the sweet viburnum as possible (for example, it is also called nannyberry and wild raisin; it bears small, purple fruits in autumn; the fruits are eaten by a variety of birds and mammals, including cardinals, partridge, gray squirrels, black bears, and opportunistic humans; white-tailed deer browse its twigs and foliage; it prefers moist, sunny areas, such as abandoned pastures, hedgerows, and woodland edges; and it is sometimes planted as an ornamental). Equipped with this knowledge and drawn by memories of its pleasant fragrance, the hiker returns to the woods seeking the sweet viburnum. After locating a healthy stand of the shrubs, he or she sniffs the flowers with abandon and then relaxes downwind of them.

Event. An event is an instance of appreciation, and it always involves *someone* appreciating *something*. In our example, the event is a hiker appreciating the sweet viburnum. Note that the emphasis on both the appreciator and the thing being appreciated prevents qualitative natural history from lapsing into subjective mood-making. The appreciator's feelings may be subjective, but the thing being appreciated is as objective as anything dealt with by scientists, and to the extent that the appreciator is able to establish a correspondence between it and his or her feelings, an instance of appreciating is objective. The skilled appreciator establishes this correspondence by identifying and then paying attention to only those feelings that can be traced to qualities in the thing being appreciated. In other words, qualitative natural history is not a mere head-game; it's an attempt to experience and respond appropriately to the *objective* qualities of natural objects and occurrences—the qualities that go right on being what they are no matter what you think about them.

If you don't automatically discount the emotional aspects of your woodland experiences, you'll discover that nature has objective emotional qualities as well as objective physical qualities. That may sound a bit loony to you, because you were probably taught that nature is cooly mechanical and value free. But attributing emotional qualities to nature is a lot less loony than assuming that all the joy of a spring morning is in your head. As philosopher John Dewey explains in *Art As Experience* (see Recommended Reading):

> The live animal does not have to project emotions into the objects experienced. Nature is kind and hateful, bland and morose, irritating and comforting, long before she is mathematically qualified or even a congeries of "secondary" qualities like colors and shapes. . . . How could it be otherwise? Direct experience comes from nature and man interacting with each other. In this interaction, human energy gathers, is released, dammed up, frustrated and victorious. There are rhythmic beats of want and fulfillment, pulses of doing and being withheld from doing.

They're slippery, but emotional qualities must be taken into account. In order to avoid unwarranted anthropomorphizing when doing so, however, when you attribute an emotional quality to an experienced object or occurrence, explain how to make the experience happen again. That way other naturalists will be able to repeat the experience and then refute or corroborate your findings. Hostility, for example, is an emotional quality of white-faced hornets who have been disturbed at the nest. If you doubt it, try fondling an active nest. You'll immediately discover just how objective an emotional quality can be. (Having been stung both indoors and out,

Thoreau was well aware that nature contains "all the qualities that can adorn a household.")

Our hiker seems to have been responding to the objective qualities of the sweet viburnum: anyone following in his or her footsteps would probably undergo a similar experience, unless purely personal reasons prevented him or her from doing so. This would not have been the case if our hiker had been attracted to the sweet viburnum because he or she had once found a $5 bill under one. There may be nothing wrong with being attracted to $5 bills, but it does change the object of the appreciating event from the sweet viburnum to paper money. The point is that it's easy to get distracted out there, so when you're in the field appreciating something, ask yourself just what it is you're appreciating (What's the event?), and whether or not the experience you're having is open to others (Am I responding to the objective qualities of the event?).

Meanings. Meaning is created when one thing is made to stand for something else. This occurred when feelings of pleasure and attraction were made to stand for the presence of white flowers, again when the tall shrub was made to stand for a member of the species sweet viburnum, and yet again when the sweet viburnum was seen as a wildlife food plant. Intelligent connection making of this sort is a no-holds-barred operation in which appropriate knowledge from the sciences, the humanities, and any other source may be used to enrich the appreciating event. Thoreau referred to this step as "making nature signify."

That meanings are essential to nature appreciation is easily overlooked; because so much of what we deal with has been meaningful to us for so long, we often fail to recognize the contributions that meanings make to our experiences. In this sense, meaning is the salt of our experiential bread. But unlike salt, meanings are artificial, the results of human intelligence and inquiry; however, we sometimes mistake meanings for integral parts of objects and occurrences. For example, "sweet viburnum" isn't the intrinsic name of those tall shrubs. It's just what we have decided to call them, and though the plant to which "sweet viburnum" points is natural, the concept "sweet viburnum" is artificial. Thus, we are responsible for making meanings. And if we own up to that responsibility, we can make our woodland experiences as meaningful, and thereby as rich, as possible.

Feelings. In addition to identifying feelings and tracing them to objective qualities in the objects and occurrences being appreciated, the qualitative naturalist also takes steps to amplify the sensations that make qualities apparent. This is a creative process in which appropriate techniques are developed and used. Our hiker used several simple techniques, including sniffing the flowers and relaxing downwind of them. But he or she could have borrowed a more sophisticated technique from wine connoisseurs, who use tulip-shaped glasses to trap volatile odors. Even the most subtly scented spring wildflower will give your winter-weary nose a jolt if you place several of its blossoms in a tulip-shaped wine glass or brandy snifter, cover the top with one hand, heat the bottom with the other, and then take three quick sniffs.

Felt-Significance. Felt-significance, the goal of qualitative natural history, occurs when meanings and feelings merge in human experience. Although felt-significance can and often does occur in the normal course of daily events, what is important here is that with adequate preparation a skilled appreciator can trigger it, just as the hiker in our example did. Initially, our hiker felt only a naive attraction for the sweet viburnum's fragrance. Then he or she took steps to make the fragrance meaningful. Finally, drawn by pleasant memories and equipped with fresh meanings, the hiker returned to the sweet viburnum and deliberately luxuriated in its fragrance, both *knowing* and *feeling* it in a way that consummated the entire episode. That's felt-significance.

No doubt you've experienced felt-significance in a variety of circumstances. Sometimes it occurs when new feelings merge with existing meanings, and at other times it occurs when new meanings merge with existing feelings, but however it occurs, it is always accompanied by the realization that you suddenly "know" something in a radically more complete way than you did before. For example, let's assume that after careful study you've purchased a paring knife. In terms of meanings, you know that the knife was skillfully made of the finest materials. Then you slice into a ripe tomato, and as paper-thin slices pile up on the cutting board, you get the feel of the knife. Feelings merge with meanings and felt-significance occurs. Now you both know and feel the good of your new knife. Or perhaps things happen the other way around. You pick up a paring knife at a friend's house and use it to prepare a salad. In the process, you acquire a feel for the knife, and it feels sharp. Then your friend adds meaning by telling you that the knife was hand-forged of high-carbon steel, hollow ground on a 2-foot grindstone, and honed by a retired brain surgeon. "Ah," you say with obvious satisfaction, "this *is* a sharp knife!" The episode has been consummated: you've experienced felt-significance.

Whether they occur when appreciating nature or in other situations, experiences of felt-significance tend to be relatively intense because the elements involved combine synergistically. Meanings and feelings magnify each other: feelings give meanings the power to move us, and meanings give feelings a focus and therefore the power to satisfy rather than merely to agitate. There is also the exercise of creative power, which occurs as circumstances are manipulated so that objects and occurrences may be experienced intelligently, and this involves the appreciator in events as nothing else can. Work and play notwithstanding, it might be said that a human being is most fully alive when he or she is appreciating something.

Although there is nothing strange or unnatural about felt-significance, it may seem so because of the way many of us have learned to separate meanings and feelings in our daily lives. Much of what we do that has obvious meaning, we do with little or no feeling, and much of what we do with obvious feeling, has little or no meaning. (Ah, if only my job *felt* as good as my hobbies, and my hobbies *meant* as much as my job.) This is "quiet desperation" in spades, but qualitative natural history counters it by uniting thinking, feeling, and acting in the service of nature appreciation.

To say that felt-significance is satisfying may be misleading. It is not meant to imply that all experiences of felt-significance are marked by happiness and joy. Some are marked by unhappiness and sorrow. In keeping with the Latin root of "satisfy," *satisfacere*, experiences of felt-significance "do enough" to exercise the complex of faculties and emotions that make one fully human. There is, however, a cost involved. A fool incapable of grasping meanings might be happily amused by the sights and sounds of a fiery tanker wreck and the consequent oil spill. But a fully developed person witnessing the same event would experience the intense sorrow that comes with connecting the sights and sounds of such a disaster with the devastating effects it will have on the habitats involved. Still, in a broad sense, this unhappy experience will satisfy the fully developed individual.

To put the matter another way, nature appreciation is a deliberate and sophisticated activity, whereas liking is a naive emotion. And although liking often plays a part in appreciation, you don't have to like something to appreciate it. There are satisfactions to be had in contemplating rotting carcasses as well as tottering fawns.

APPLICATION

In summary, then, the goal of qualitative natural history is felt significance, and it is achieved by (1) identifying the appreciating event, (2) making the object or occurrence being appreciated meaningful, (3) identifying and amplifying the sensations and emotions associated with the appreciated object or occurrence, and (4) providing opportunities for meanings and feelings to merge during consummatory experiences in which the appreciated object or occurrence is directly involved. You've probably been operating along these lines already, even if you haven't thought about the process in this way. In any case, the next time you're appreciating something in the woods, see if you can identify the event, meanings, feelings, and felt-significance involved, as well as the meaning-making techniques, sensory techniques, and consummatory experiences you're using. If there is an element missing or in short supply, correct the deficiency and watch the quality of your experience change for the better. While you're at it, see how many of the elements and techniques you can identify in each of the excursions described in Chapters 6 through 10

The Good of Qualitative Natural History

With so many environmental problems confronting us, some may feel that it's irresponsible to concentrate on nature appreciation. This is tantamount to scoring the chef who pauses to savor a soup in the making. In order to know what, if anything, ought to be added, the chef must be able to appreciate what is already there. Similarly, there is a necessary connection between intelligent appreciation and the wise management of natural resources. In many areas we have the technical know-how to get what we want, but we don't know what we *ought* to want. Skill in appreciating nature can help us in choosing worthy environmental goals.

Qualitative natural history also recommends itself to concerned environmentalists because of the *kind* of activity it is. As conservationist Aldo Leopold (*A Sand County Almanac: With Other Essays on Conservation from Round River*. New York: Oxford University Press, 1966) wrote:

> It would appear, in short, that the rudimentary grades of outdoor recreation consume their resource-base; the higher grades, at least to a degree, create their own satisfactions with little or no attrition of land or life.

Qualitative natural history is one of the "higher grades" of outdoor recreation.

Finally, in an industrial society, where everything is seen as a means to something else, we need resting places, and qualitative natural history can supply them. It does so by demonstrating—through the experience of felt-significance—that wild apples, waterfalls, and woodchucks can be experienced as ends. If one knows how to appreciate them, they can satisfy.

Conclusion

"Okay," you say, "but do you have to be a connoisseur to appreciate nature, can't you just enjoy it the way most people enjoy wine?"

Sure you can, and many people do, but if you approach nature as a connoisseur, your experiences will be richer, you'll be able to sustain your interest longer, and you'll probably make less destructive demands on the environment. It pays to take responsibility for the quality of your experiences afield.

As you read through the remaining chapters, you'll see that they contain general information and specific activities designed to acquaint you with the more practical aspects of qualitative natural history. The theoretical terminology used in this chapter will not, for the most part, appear again. The chapters that follow, however, are based on the method described above, and they will enable you to experience the kind of satisfaction that expert nature appreciators have always enjoyed.

Recommended Reading

AMERINE, MAYNARD A. and ROESSLER, EDWARD B. *Wines: Their Sensory Evaluation.* San Francisco: W. H. Freeman and Co., 1976. An in-depth introduction to the mechanics behind the oldest continuing tradition of connoisseurship involving a seminatural product. Many of the concepts and principles explained here can be applied to natural objects and occurrences.

BAILEY, LIBERTY HYDE. *The Holy Earth.* New York: Charles Scribner's Sons, 1915; reprint edition, Ithaca, New York: New York State College of Agriculture and Life Sciences, 1980. An eloquent statement on the need to establish an appreciative relationship with the earth and its products. You'll probably have to ask your local bookstore to order it, but you won't be sorry you did.

DEWEY, JOHN. *Art As Experience.* New York: G. P. Putnam's Sons, 1934; reprint edition, New York: Paragon Books, 1979. This book is about the intelligent appreciation of works of art, but nature appreciators will find the following chapters helpful: "The Live Creature," "The Live Creature and 'Etherial Things'," "Having an Experience," and "Criticism and Perception."

GOWIN, D. BOB. *Educating.* Ithaca, New York: Cornell University Press, 1981. Educators interested in the role felt-significance plays in education will find this book of interest. Professor Gowin puts forth a theory of education that may change the way you think about the process.

PEPI, DAVID A. "Regularities in Exemplar Cases of Environmental Appreciating." Ph.D. dissertation, Cornell University, 1982. Xerographic copies available from University Microfilms International, 300 N. Zeeb Road, Ann Arbor, Michigan 48106. Those who want proof that Thoreau, Muir, and other first-rate nature appreciators used a common method will find this of interest. It also contains a more detailed explanation of the method and its similarities to wine connoisseurship.

CHAPTER TWO
Clothing and Gear

Go light; the lighter the better, so that you have the simplest material for health, comfort and enjoyment.

"Nessmuk"
Woodcraft and Camping, 1920

Dressing for the Woods

The art of dressing for the woods consists of striking a balance between protection and perception. In most woodland situations, the body needs at least some protection from things such as biting insects, prickly plants, and the weather. On the other hand, sense organs don't work well when covered. Your skin can't see through wool or leather any better than your eyes can. Accordingly, the first principle of dressing for the woods is to provide your sense organs with the highest degree of exposure to the environment that is consistent with good health and reasonable comfort.

Most errors are made on the side of overdressing. If your clothing is too light, you'll be cold and uncomfortable, and you'll do something about it. But if your clothing is just a bit too heavy, you may be too warm and comfortable to notice it, and you'll spend the day in your clothes rather than in the woods. An analogy from falconry may be helpful here.

Instead of making contented pets of their hawks, falconers strive to keep them alert and eager to hunt. They accomplish this by feeding the birds just enough to maintain good health, while at the same time keeping them on the hungry edge characteristic of birds in the wild. A hawk in this condition is at the height of its powers and is said to be in a state of *yarak*. Similarly, by wearing just enough clothing you can keep your senses in a state of yarak.

The second principle of dressing for the woods is to wear clothing that blends into the habitat you're visiting. A naturalist usually goes to the woods to see, not to be seen. Soft greens, browns, and tans blend into the woods better than bright reds, oranges, and yellows. (While it is true that many mammals are said to see the world in shades of gray, birds and people see colors.) In most cases, there is no need to go to extremes; on a day trip you need not look like either a derelict or a camouflaged soldier. Even the American woodcock, the master of camouflage, is a natty dresser.

During the deer hunting season the second principle doesn't apply. If you enter the woods at all during this period, you'll want to be highly visible, and you will be if you wear a blaze-orange safety vest and hat (sporting goods stores stock them just before the season opens). Blaze-orange is bright, but it's not bulletproof, so even when you are wearing it, stay clear of hunters.

What do principles one and two mean at five o'clock in the morning when you're dressing for a day afield? Consider the following situation: The day is a mild one in April or September, and you'll be hiking through a mixture of upland woods and fields. What do you wear?

FOOTWEAR

Stout leather boots with foam padding, heel counters, and lug soles may be just the ticket for mountain climbing, heavy backpacking, and logging, but they are worse than useless for doing qualitative natural history. They protect too much. Think of your feet as sense organs. If they can feel the earth, they'll tell you of the beech nuts and vole burrows beneath the leaves; in lug sole boots, all they'll tell you about are shoe nails and seams. Leave lug soles for those who need them. As a qualitative naturalist, you can afford to walk softly.

Moccasins, the indigenous footwear of North America, are a sensible alternative to heavy boots. A moccasin is a shoe made entirely of pliable leather. In its simplest form, a moccasin consists of two pieces of leather; one large piece, the *vamp*, cradles the foot, and a smaller piece, the *toe-piece*, or *plug*, is stitched to the top of the cradle to keep the moccasin on (Figure 2-1). This stitching forms the characteristic ridge found around the toes of all true moccasins and some imitations (imitations because the vamps end at the soles instead of extending under the feet to form cradles). An extra layer of leather is sometimes molded and stitched to the sole for longer wear.

True moccasins don't offer much support, water soaks through the all-leather soles, and they are so pliable you have to be careful where you place your feet. These features force you to walk alertly, and they add a new dimension to your experiences afield as your feet come alive and strike up an intimate relationship with the earth.

Most commercial moccasins rise to just below the ankle. This can cause problems: burrs and pebbles may enter the shoe and your

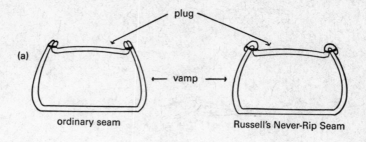

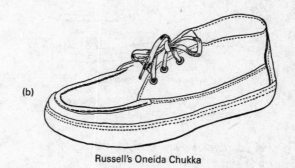

FIGURE 2-1. True moccasins, the indigenous footwear of North America: (a) cross sections of two moccasins; (b) high-topped moccasin with molded leather sole.

ankle is exposed to bruising. A local leather worker may be able to make you a pair of true moccasins with high tops, or you can order a pair from the Russell Moccasin Company of Berlin, Wisconsin (see Appendix for the addresses of companies mentioned in this chapter). Each pair they make is handcrafted and made to order the way *you* want them. Russell will send you a catalog and measuring instructions free of charge. This is a fine old company, and knowing that it still exists is as reassuring as knowing about a wilderness lake where loons still nest unmolested.

As rewarding as true moccasins are, they are not practical in all situations. You may want to reserve them for places you know and for outings where sensual contact with the earth is paramount. When there is distance to be covered over unknown or rocky ter-

Russell's Bird Shooter

FIGURE 2-2. Upland boots, true moccasins with man-made soles attached.

rain, you'll find an *upland boot*, a high moccasin with a man-made sole, just right (Figure 2-2).

When shopping for an upland boot, look for chrome or oil-tanned lightweight leather, along with rubber, crepe rubber, or knurled rubber soles and heels. Any height from 4 to 10 inches will do. Higher boots are not as well ventilated, they bind at the calf, and they weigh more. At least two companies (see Appendix) still make true moccasin-style upland boots and several companies make good imitations.

Your leather boots and moccasins will last longer and serve you better if you treat them regularly with a waterproofing compound. Wax-based compounds will not cause leather to stretch or become overly soft as some oils and greases will. If you have shoe trees, use them when you waterproof your boots and when you store them. They keep boots in shape when you're working on them, and they prevent creases from developing into cracks when boots are stored.

Apply waterproofing compound when your boots or moccasins are warm and dry, being sure to coat all leather surfaces, especially the dark cranny where the vamp of an upland boot meets the sole. Let the treated footwear rest awhile in a warm spot; then work the compound into the leather with your hands. Waterproofing boots and moccasins is a messy and satisfying ritual, but don't think for a moment that it will make them waterproof. It might make them water-resistant, and it will definitely make them last longer.

For a mixture of wet and dry terrain, the L. L. Bean Company of Freeport, Maine, makes the Maine Hunting Shoe, a cross between a pair of rubbers and a pair of leather boots (Figure 2-3). These hybrids are light, have excellent traction, and the soles are pliable enough to keep your feet awake. A pair of felt insoles will

FIGURE 2-3. Footwear for wet walking in April and September: (a) the L. L. Bean Maine Hunting Shoe, 10 inches; (b) the Uniroyal pull-on boot in neoprene, 12 inches.

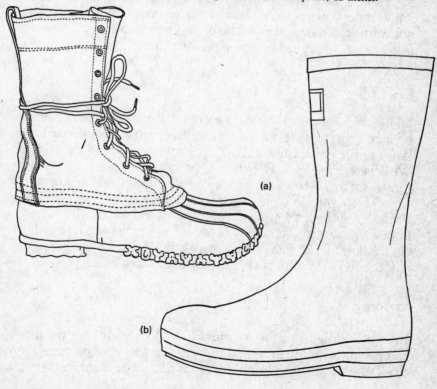

keep boots of this type from becoming too clammy, and you can keep your socks from creeping off by folding the tops of the socks over the outsides of the boots.

When the going is very wet and you want to keep your feet dry, try rubber boots. A quality pair—such as those made by Uniroyal—with 10-inch tops and snug-fitting ankles will keep your feet dry, and they won't slip at the heel with each step (Figure 2-3). To their surprise, some hikers find that all-rubber boots of this type do not get as clammy as the leather-rubber hybrids. Having no laces, the top of an all rubber boot fits loosely, allowing air to circulate through the boot with each step.

In situations where you can enjoy being wet—summertime ponds, swamps, and streams—the trout fisherman's nylon wading shoes work well. High-top sneakers work almost as well, and if you don't mind having to fish them out of the mud occasionally, old tennis shoes will do. Going barefoot is tempting, but in most places not worth the risk; a glass bottle or two has been broken since the first Europeans arrived on the North American continent.

PANTS

Short pants are a treat in mild weather when biting insects are few, because they provide for sensory contact with one of the lower layers of the environment that might otherwise go unappreciated. With bare legs you'll feel the elasticity of the black and yellow garden spider's web and the caress of the sapling white pine.

When you do wear long pants, let them hang outside your boots. If you tuck them inside, rain, dew, and seeds will be drawn from your pants to your socks. Short or long, pants ought to be fully cut to allow for freedom of movement and air circulation. For loose, airy comfort, some hikers prefer suspenders to a belt.

SHIRTS

In mild weather a cotton T-shirt with a pocket for your notebook and pencil is practical. When the weather gets cool or buggy, top the T-shirt with a long-sleeve, cotton flannel or wool shirt.

(a)

(b)

FIGURE 2-4. Vests for warmth and pockets: (a) Eddie Bauer Downlight Canadian Vest; (b) Filson Cruiser Vest.

VESTS

There are two good reasons to wear a vest: warmth and pockets. For warmth you can't beat the kind of goose-down vest that is worn over a shirt but under a jacket. These vests are comfortably snug-fitting, lightweight, and they don't take much room in a day pack. You may want to carry one with you in all but the hottest weather. Eddie Bauer's Downlight Canadian Vest (Figure 2-4) has been manufactured for almost fifty years, and not without reason.

For pockets a _cruiser vest_ is ideal. These vests were designed to keep handy the maps, compass, notebook, and pencil of the timber cruiser (a forester who roams the woods estimating the amount of timber present and marking trees to be cut by logging crews). A cruiser vest is covered inside and out, front and back, with pockets. The Filson Company of Seattle, Washington, makes the traditional cruiser vest (Figure 2-4), and they'll sell you one by mail or you can order one from a forestry supply house. These cotton duck vests will last indefinitely, and after three or four years of sun and rain, yours will fade to a natural tan that will make a hillside of dry grass envious.

JACKETS

Look for the following features in a lightweight jacket: a tailored collar rather than an attached hood (in mild weather hoods are too confining and they are branch-catching nuisances when not in use), slash pockets for your hands, and enough length to keep your lower back covered when you bend over. (In catalogs the terms "jacket," "coat," and "parka" are used loosely. Technically, a jacket covers *only* the upper half of the body, a coat covers *at least* the upper half, and a parka has a hood. So what we're actually talking about here are field coats.) A light jacket used in combination with a down vest, a long-sleeve shirt, and a T-shirt will get you from April to October. Add a dark green waterproof poncho, or a long-length waterproof parka, and you'll be prepared for wet weather as well. A poncho can also be used as a ground cloth when you're looking for a dry place to sit in the woods. Carry the items you're not wearing in your pack. In April and September you often have to face two or three seasons a day.

HATS

Few things are as satisfying as looking out at a gentle rain from beneath a snap-brim, felt hat, or fedora. The best felt hats are made of beaver fur and have leather sweatbands. Unlike wool felt, beaver felt will not shrink after a soaking; and when a leather sweatband gets dirty, you can wipe it clean. A hat with a crown of at least $4\frac{1}{2}$ inches, a $2\frac{1}{4}$ to $2\frac{1}{2}$ inch brim snapped down all around with a little upward flair over the ears, and grommets on either side of the crown for ventilation will serve you well in spring and fall (Figure 2-5). In hot summer weather a similarly shaped straw hat—with a leather sweatband—will keep you cool as a cuke.

When you don't want it on your head, a beaver-felt hat can be an inconvenience, because it's a travesty to stuff one in your day pack. Moreover, beaver-felt hats are tough on beavers. One alternative is a cotton poplin cap with a visor. These are not as good in the rain, and they don't protect your ears or the back of your neck from the sun, but when you want to feel the wind in your hair, you can stick a cap in your pack. Caps are also convenient when you're

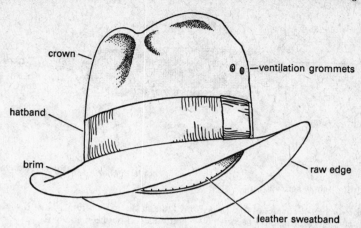

FIGURE 2-5. A snap brim, beaver-felt hat with a leather sweatband.

lying down on a hillside or in a meadow; there is no back brim to get in your way and the visor can be positioned to shade your eyes during reveries.

Gear: Going Light

If even a thin line existed between those items properly thought of as necessary equipment and those items properly thought of as impediments, packing for a day hike would require little thought. Unfortunately, no such line exists. Your own critical judgment will have to be applied on an item-by-item basis. In making your decisions, you may find it helpful to bear the following two axioms in mind: (1) of the many things you might take on a day hike, none can compare with a light pack and an easy mind, (2) don't take it, and you won't have to carry it.

Some of the items that you do bring will depend on the day's activity. For example, a day spent on a mountain top watching migrating hawks will require different gear from that used for a day spent in a bog investigating pitcher plants. Nonetheless, there are certain core items that you'll want to have with you each time you enter the woods. An item of this type is called a *vade mecum*, from the Latin meaning "go with me."

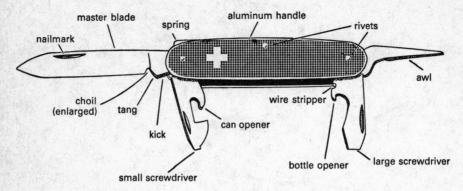

FIGURE 2-6. Pioneer model of the Swiss Army knife made by Victorinox. Note that the brass fin and lanyard ring have been removed and the choil has been enlarged.

JACKKNIVES

Choosing a Jackknife. The jackknife is the quintessential vade mecum. It will slice a wild apple crosswise to reveal the star, expose tapeworms in the gut of a road-killed woodchuck, and make a willow whistle. Jackknives range from sleek, long-bladed trapper's models with nickel-silver bolsters and bone handles, to bulky, many-bladed combination knives.

Some purists claim that the only good jackknives are the ones with only one or two cutting blades. "If you carry a combination knife," say the purists, "you carry a bad knife, a bad screwdriver, and a bad bottle opener." This argument has some merit, and it's worth pursuing over a bottle of ale or two—as long as one of the advocates has a combination knife to open the bottles. Carry a quality jackknife of almost any style, and you'll grow fond of it with use.

One of the most practical combination jackknives available is the aluminum-handled model of the Swiss Army Knife made by Victorinox and variously referred to as the Sturdy Boy and Pioneer (Figure 2-6). It has four blades: (1) a large cutting blade, (2) a large screwdriver/cap lifter/wire stripper (the wire stripper is the little notch at the base of the blade), (3) a small screwdriver/can opener, and (4) an awl. The awl opens at one end of the knife, rather than in the middle as in other models, making it easier to use as an awl or a probe. In addition, the Pioneer is more durable than the more costly models made by Victorinox: the handles are made of metal rather than plastic, the center scale (the thin piece of metal used to separate the springs and blades) is made of brass rather than aluminum, the rivets are made of stainless steel rather than a softer metal, and the stainless steel blades, though not as highly polished as in other models, are made of thicker stock. With hard use, a plastic-handled Swiss Army Knife will serve you daily for years before it loosens and falls apart; the less expensive Pioneer will serve you daily until you lose it.

You can buy jackknives through the mail, but this is not recommended. Go to a store that stocks them, and ask the salesperson to put at least three jackknives of the make and model you want to buy on the counter. Examine each of them; then choose the best one on the basis of the following tests:

1. Open the large cutting blade. Hold the sides of the blade with the fingers of one hand and hold the handle with the fingers of your other hand. Try to jiggle the blade from side to side. If it moves, don't buy it.

2. If they are visible, check the rivets that hold the knife together. They should be firmly and evenly set.

3. Open each blade/tool. Each should move smoothly to the three-quarter open position. Then it should snap into the fully open position, seating itself with an uncompromising click. (The large screwdriver on the Pioneer also clicks and seats firmly in the half-open position, so it can be used in tight places.)

4. If the handles have insets of antler, wood, or plastic, check to see if they abut the metal ends of the handles (bolsters) cleanly and with no gaps. A gap filled with gray epoxy is still a gap, and it may eventually cause the handle to loosen and fall off.

5. Finally, place the closed knife on its back and look straight down on the blades and tools. It's a close fit in there, but each blade should just clear the others.

Modifying Your Jackknife. If you buy a Swiss Army Knife, you may want to remove the lanyard ring and the brass fin to which it is attached. Otherwise, these protuberances will jab your palm and rob you of the sensual pleasure that comes from holding and using a good jackknife. Besides, the place to carry a jackknife is in your pocket, or better yet, in a small, leather belt-sheath. Slip off the lanyard ring, then file away the brass fin using a fine file. Before you begin filing, cover the end of the jackknife's handles with masking tape so you won't scratch them.

As long as you have your file out, you may also want to increase the size of the master blade's *choil,* the small notch between the blade's cutting edge and *kick* (the kick is the leading edge of the *tang,* the thick, unground portion of the blade that enters and is attached to the handle). Do this with a triangular file or use a flat file with a sharpened edge held diagonally. A choil one-eighth of an inch deep and three-sixteenths of an inch from cutting edge to kick will enable you to run the blade along a sharpening stone smoothly and without rounding off the edge of your stone with the kick (Figure 2-6). Of course, the bigger choil increases the chances of breaking the master blade when you use it as a lever, but it's not supposed to be used as a lever anyway. That's what the large screwdriver is for.

Sharpening a Jackknife. One of the pleasures of owning a jackknife is sharpening it. No doubt you have, or soon will develop, your own knife-sharpening technique. If you're new at it, you may want to proceed as follows. First, obtain a sharpening stone that is at least 8 inches long, 2 inches wide, and 1 inch thick. Stones of this size and larger are called *bench stones,* because they are used while on a workbench or table. The extra length will enable you to take long, smooth strokes, and the extra thickness will keep your knuckles from scraping the table as you take them.

There are many kinds of bench stones from which to choose, each of which has certain advantages. However, a combination India stone, coarse grit on one side and fine grit on the other, is a wise choice for the beginner. India stones are made of aluminum oxide and they are brown in color. A combination India stone will not last as long or give you the surgical edge that a set of natural Arkansas stones will, but a combination India stone costs much less, and it will cut steel faster, so you can easily monitor your results as you perfect your technique. A set of Japanese water stones will produce a keener edge than a combination India stone, but again, a quality set of Japanese water stones is more costly. The Carborundum stones that are common in hardware stores soak up oil and they have a generally unpleasant feel under the knife.

When you're ready to sharpen your jackknife, sit at a kitchen table or stand at a workbench and place the stone before you, coarse side up and perpendicular to the table's near edge. If possible, the stone should be immobilized by nailing a half-inch thick block of wood to the bench top at each end of the stone. This setup will leave your hands free to manipulate the knife (Figure 2-7).

During the actual sharpening process, the angle at which the blade is held to the stone is everything. To determine that angle, lay the blade flat on the far end of the stone, cutting edge toward you, and a source of light somewhere above and behind the knife. Bend down, and you'll see a black line, a shadow, between the cutting edge of the blade and the stone. Hold the knife by the

FIGURE 2-7. A jackknife positioned for a sharpening stroke on a bench stone.

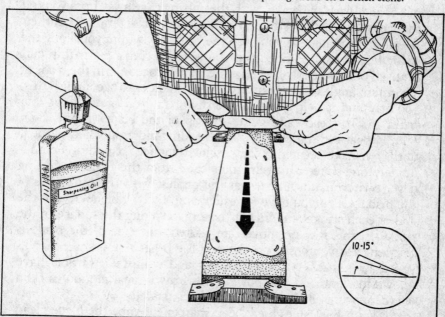

handle with one hand, and twist your wrist so as to raise the back edge of the blade above the stone. As you do so, the black line will grow thinner. When it disappears, the cutting edge of the blade is in contact with the surface of the stone. That's the angle at which you'll want to hold the knife throughout the sharpening process. At most, the back of the blade will be a quarter of an inch above the stone, and the blade will be at an angle of from 10° to 15°. That's not much of an angle. What you're after is a gently tapered, thin cutting edge.

Now squirt a generous dollop of *sharpening* oil on the stone and use your knife to spread it over the entire surface. This pool of oil will keep particles of steel, or *swarf*, from glazing the stone's cutting surface. Sharpening oils are light oils. If you use a more viscous oil, it will prevent glazing, but it may decrease your stone's ability to abrade steel. In addition, good sharpening oils are non-toxic, an important consideration when sharpening knives that come in contact with food.

Once the stone has been oiled, hold your jackknife with one hand, and place the blade, with the cutting edge away from you, on the near end of the stone at the angle you determined earlier. Maintain that angle as you push the blade away from you along the entire length of the stone, as if you were shaving a paper-thin curl from a block of clear basswood. The trick is to maintain the blade at a constant angle throughout the stroke. In order to accomplish this, you may find it helpful to use the thumb and/or forefinger of your free hand to steady and guide the tip of the blade (Figure 2-7).

Repeat the sharpening stroke, adding more oil when needed, until you have created a flat, angular surface extending approximately one-sixteenth of an inch back from the extreme cutting edge. Switch hands and repeat the process with the other side of the blade. Or, if you have a steady hand, flip the blade over at the end of each stroke and draw it toward you along the surface of the stone. In this way no moves are wasted; one side of the blade is sharpened as you push it away, and the other side is sharpened as you draw it back. As craftspersons and cold-steel warriors have known for centuries, the power of this rhythmical motion to calm and center oneself is not to be underestimated.

When both sides have been sharpened, wipe the blade clean

of oil, grit, and swarf, turn the stone over, and repeat the entire process using the fine side of the stone. Stop occasionally and pass the tip of your thumbnail across the blade, from the back to the cutting edge. Do this on both sides of the blade, and on one side, the side that was away from the stone on the last stroke, you'll feel a slight ridge, or _wire edge_, along the cutting edge. This ridge is formed of partially attached particles of steel. You can remove it by taking a few very light strokes on each side of the blade after you've put an edge on it.

When the wire edge has been removed and the cutting edge of the blade won't slide off a thumbnail held at a 45° angle, your knife is sharp. And when it will cleanly shave a moistened patch of hair from your forearm, it's very sharp, but you'll probably have to use a hard Arkansas stone, a Japanese _Shiage Toishi_ (polishing stone), or a leather strop to get it that way.

CANTEEN

In some remote parts of North America, one of the joys of a day afield is the cool taste of woodland water. But if you're in an area where potable water is not readily available in the woods, carry a canteen in your day pack. If you can't find one with a leakproof cap, try a polyethylene laboratory bottle. Biological supply houses and some mail order outfitters stock them. In moderate weather, a pint-size bottle is adequate for one person; if you're with a friend, take two pint-size bottles. They'll pack more comfortably than one quart bottle. When it's hot out, the juice of a fresh lemon makes even warm water refreshing.

CONTAINERS

Occasionally you'll come across a shrew's skull, the abandoned nest of a ruby-throated hummingbird, or some other woodland bijou that you want to enjoy at home. Therefore, it's a good idea to keep two screw-top, wide-mouth, polyethylene jars in your pack, one with a diameter of about 2 inches, the other with a diameter of about 3 inches, and both about 2 or 3 inches high. Stuff a small plastic bag in one, a large plastic bag in the other, and you'll be ready for anything that presents itself.

FIRE

Fire-making capability is a good thing to have in the woods whether you use it or not. Carry matches in a waterproof container or carry a butane lighter. The lighter will work when wet.

TAPE MEASURE

Lay a tape on anything that will stand still for it. A record of a red oak with a circumference of 18 feet is more meaningful than a record of a "very large" red oak. This is especially true if you can compare it to records you have made of other red oaks. The cloth tape measures sold in sewing shops work well, but the 10-foot tapes sold by forestry and scientific supply houses are handier because they come in steel cases with push-button returns. A steel carpenter's tape will not do because most of them have concave tape lines designed to stay rigid when extended, and this makes them hard to wrap around objects. In the field, a flat, flexible tape-line is best.

THERMOMETER

Does the skunk cabbage really melt its way through the spring snow with a heated flower bud? You might be able to find out if you carry a thermometer in the woods. Cased pocket thermometers are available from forestry supply houses and from some mail-order outfitters. The cases have clips, so you can carry and lose these thermometers like pens. Thermometers filled with red liquid usually have lower minimum temperatures than mercury-filled thermometers—a handy feature in the north country. Some retailers who serve mountain climbers stock pocket-size thermometers that record the lowest temperature reached between settings. Tied to a line, one of these *minimum register thermometers* will tell you how cold the water is down there, and tied to the end of a flexible willow wand, a minimum register thermometer will tell you how cool it is inside a woodchuck's burrow.

INSECT REPELLENT

A 1-ounce bottle of liquid insect repellent is worth carrying when biting insects are out. *N,N-diethyl-meta-toluamide*, or *deet*, is the active ingredient that seems to be most effective. (What deet does to the human body, I don't know.) Generally, the more deet in a repellent, the better the repellent. You may, however, want to consider such things as ease of application and container design. Lotions, for example, are easier to handle than less viscous fluids, and a small, unbreakable bottle with a flip-top nozzle will fit comfortably in your shirt pocket, and it has no cap to lose.

Common sense suggests that deet be used only when necessary; therefore, there is a tendency to suffer several insect bites before applying it. This approach will leave you with insect bites *and* a dose of deet. Instead, try to anticipate buggy situations and apply the repellent before you need it.

Be careful. Some insect repellents wreak havoc on coated lenses. If you wipe your repellent-protected brow with a handkerchief, don't use that same handkerchief to brush pollen off your binocular's lenses.

DOG REPELLENT

When hiking in settled country, where woodland paths all too often lead to backyards guarded by faithful dogs, dog repellent is a comfort. Fortunately, it is almost always possible to avoid canine confrontations by walking an extra mile, cutting through a swamp rather than walking the trail, or leaving the field entirely. But when a confrontation can't be avoided and you are about to be bitten, a pocket-size can of "Halt!" dog repellent may enable you to escape uninjured.

"Halt!" comes in an aerosol can that squirts a thin stream of liquid repellent up to 10 feet. Capsaicin, which is found in paprika, is the active ingredient. The repellent is advertised as being "temporarily painful, but medically safe." Your mail carrier or meter reader can probably tell you how effective it is. "Halt!" is available from forestry supply houses and from some bicycle shops. Ask for it if you don't see it on display; it's often kept under the counter. I've carried the same three-quarter-ounce can of "Halt!" for eight years and haven't used it yet, but there have been times when it felt good in my pocket.

A woodswoman I know chides me for carrying "Halt!" She speaks "dog" and claims that she can handle even vicious dogs by assuming their dominance posture: head erect and ears perked straight up. She uses her hands for ears, one on either side of her head, hands open, palms to the dog. The only drawback to this technique is that it requires raw courage. For many of us, "Halt!" is easier to come by.

DAY PACK

Some vade mecums, such as your notebook and pencil, are best carried in your pocket where you can get at them easily; bulky and seldom-used items go in a day pack. For a serviceable day pack, choose one with the following features: Cordura nylon construction, padded shoulder straps, nylon top loop for hand carrying and hanging, a coil-zippered main compartment, and an outside center pocket with a covered coil zipper. As with other articles of clothing and gear, a day pack's color should blend with the out-of-doors.

Once you get used to wearing a small pack, it will feel as comfortable as your favorite hiking shirt. And you can keep it that way, even when it's fully loaded, by packing your folded poncho, down vest, or jacket so as to form a cushion between yourself and back-jabbers such as field guides and canteens.

WALKING STICK

In *The New Complete Walker*, Colin Fletcher says that in rough terrain a walking stick converts him from an "insecure biped to a confident triped." On the other hand, in *Ways of the Woods*,

William M. Harlow mentions that he doesn't use one himself and notes that "I've never seen even one old Adirondack guide (unless crippled) using a cane or a staff." The choice is up to you.

In terms of qualitative natural history, a walking stick makes an excellent probe, and it's just the thing to knock down a wild apple or fish a dead muskrat out of a pond. If you do decide to carry one, don't let someone else rob you of the pleasure of finding it. Somewhere out there a walking stick awaits you, and like a guru, it will appear before you when you're ready for it.

Hickory, hop-hornbeam, American hornbeam, and white ash make rugged sticks, but many other woods will do. I use a staghorn sumac stick that presented itself to me when it was dead, dry, and free of bark. It's much lighter than the stronger woods mentioned above, and thanks to a bittersweet vine that grew around it, there is a grooved, spiral ridge running its length. Crooked, knotty, deeply textured sticks of this sort are a pleasure to carry; a smooth, machine-finished stick is a bore.

If you're going to cut your stick from a living tree and you plan to peel the bark off, cut the stick in late spring or early summer. If you want the bark to stay on, cut your stick in the winter.

OTHER VADE MECUMS

A number of important items that you'll want to have along on most trips have been dealt with in other chapters. Those items and chapters are as follows: notebook and pencil, Chapter 5; binoculars, hand lens, and field guides, Chapter 3; topographic maps and compass, Chapter 4.

Conclusion

The equipment discussed above constitutes a qualitative naturalist's basic field kit for mild weather. You may wish to add, delete, and/or modify items, depending on where and why you do your walking. This is as it should be. In time you'll evolve a distinctly personal set of gear, and if you store it in one place, you'll be able to pack, dress, and be out the door before you can come up with a good reason not to go.

Thought Questions

1. In *The Maine Woods*, Thoreau lists the components of a "good outfit" for twelve days in the outdoors during July. One of the items he recommends is a pair of gloves. Why?

Hint: Squeeze bottles of deet were not available in the 1840s.

2. William M. Harlow, emeritus professor of wood technology at the SUNY College of Environmental Sciences and Forestry at Syracuse University, writing in the August 1977 issue of *Backpacker*, states:

> Take nothing but photos, leave nothing but footprints. This familiar slogan is fine as far as it goes, but if you really want to preserve the environment, you'd better take a second look at those footprints you're leaving.

Dr. Harlow goes on to recommend the use of footwear with plain soles, as opposed to footwear with lug soles, or "waffle stompers." What do boot soles have to do with preserving woodland environments?

Hint: You might want to repeat an experiment Dr. Harlow conducted. Fill a box with sandy loam soil; then make two boot-sole impressions in the soil, one with a lug sole and the other with a plain sole. Place the box outside at a 20°-angle during a rainy day or night. Compare the amount of erosion that occurs at each impression.

You can arrive at an answer to this question another way. Consider the ground-cover plants that protect forest soils from erosion. Then consider the following question posed by Dr. Harlow: "If you were kicked in the face with a boot, would you rather it were flat-bottomed or covered with sharp-edged little blocks three-eighths of an inch long?"

3. At a certain time of the year, using a white handkerchief in the woods can be deadly. When and why?

Hint: Picture a white-tailed deer bounding away from a hunter—white tail waving. Now picture a white handkerchief being drawn with a flourish from pocket to face.

4. Knife makers say that a *good* jackknife "walks and talks." What do they mean?

Hint: The blades of a good jackknife move easily and they click into place.

5. Many people who use knives regularly prefer moderately hard steel blades, rather than the super-hard steel blades one sees advertised in some outdoor catalogs. Why?

Hint: No matter how hard a blade is, if it's used often, it will get dull often. Regular users find that the increased edge-holding ability of the super-hard blades does not outweigh the increased time and effort it takes to put an edge on them, so they use blades of softer steel that can be sharpened with a few quick strokes.

Recommended Reading

BRAND, STEWART, ed. *The Next Whole Earth Catalog: Access to Tools.* New York: Random House, 1980. A good place to look for manufacturers and suppliers of outdoor gear and clothing. See also the sections entitled "Whole Systems," "Land Use," and "Nomadics."

FLETCHER, COLIN. *The New Complete Walker.* New York: Alfred A. Knopf, 1974. This book about backpacking is *the* book to have for an introduction to outdoor gear and for an extensive list of retail suppliers. Fletcher's wit and wisdom are bonuses.

HARLOW, WILLIAM M. *Ways of the Woods.* Washington, D.C.: The American Forestry Association, 1980. This book is the next best thing to a year in the woods with an Adirondack guide. Among its many high points are the definitive directions for making a willow or moosewood whistle. See the chapters entitled "Boots and Clothing for the Woods" and "The Camper's Tools: Knife, Hatchet, Saw."

"Insect Repellents." *Consumer Reports*, June 1980, pp. 304–305. Insect repellents are discussed in general, and fifteen commercial repellents are compared in terms of cost and percentage of deet in each.

NESSMUK (GEORGE WASHINGTON SEARS). *Woodcraft and Camping.* New York: Forest and Stream Publishing Co., 1920; reprint and slightly abridged edition, New York: Dover Publications, Inc., 1963. This is the outdoor classic in which Nessmuk writes, "We do not go to the green woods and crystal waters to rough it, we go to smooth it. We get it rough enough at home. . . ." Nessmuk serves up the go-light philosophy full strength.

CHAPTER THREE
Books and Binoculars

Objects are concealed from our view, not so much because they are out of the course of our visual ray as because we do not bring our minds and eyes to bear on them, for there is no power to see in the eye itself, any more than there is in any other jelly.

Henry David Thoreau
"Autumnal Tints"
Writings, Vol. 5, 1906

An appropriately rumpled professor of philosophy at an urban university begins his class on the nature of reality with an anecdote about his young daughter. He tells of the first time they left the city for a vacation in the Maine woods. As they drove along the dirt road leading to their cabin, the professor was struck by the beauty of the pines on either side of the road, so he stopped the car, got out, lifted the child into his arms, and asked, "What do you see?" After pausing a moment to look around, the little girl replied, "Nothing!"

The point is that "seeing," as we commonly use the term, is a highly sophisticated activity. The little girl had been raised in the city where "something to see" meant a favorite store, a set of traffic lights, or a gathering of people. Given that context, there *was* nothing to see on the country road.

In this chapter we'll examine two ways to augment vision: books and binoculars. Both can be used to see new things and to see old things in new ways.

Books

CHOOSING FIELD GUIDES

There is no end to the buying of field guides. New ones are being produced constantly. Many of them don't work well in the field, and once you have several even the better ones become repetitive. Still, with very few exceptions, every field guide you can afford is worth having. Keep a few by your favorite chair and on winter nights browse through them like seed catalogs. Your memory will unconsciously lay away images and information that will serve you well in months and years to come. Many naturalists will tell you that the first time they saw a tiger beetle or dragon arum they were able to identify it—and perhaps spotted it in the first place—because they had previously seen and read about it in a field guide. In other words, the more you know, the more you see.

With experience you'll learn which guides work best in the field, and those will be the ones that you'll want to carry with you. The others will be waiting on your bookshelf to corroborate field identifications. Here are three examples of guides that are worth their weight in a pack:

1. _Birds of North America._ Chandler S. Robbins, Bertel Brunn, and Herbert S. Zim. New York: Golden Press, 1966.
2. _Newcomb's Wildflower Guide._ Lawrence Newcomb. Boston: Little, Brown and Co., 1977.
3. _Trees of the Eastern United States and Canada._ William Harlow. New York: Dover Publications, Inc., 1957.

Other excellent field guides are discussed in the Recommended Reading sections of Chapters 6 through 10.

FIELD PROOFING

Field guides carried in a pack take a beating, and if they're paperbacks, which are practical because they conform to odd spaces, they'll eventually fall apart. You can prevent this from happening by field proofing them with braided nylon fishing line and cloth tape. Here's how:

1. Place the brand-new book on a piece of plywood or an old Sears catalog, and use a $\frac{5}{64}$-inch or $\frac{3}{32}$-inch drill bit to drill a row of holes approximately three-sixteenths of an inch from the spine and half an inch apart (Figure 3-1).
2. Cut at least a yard of stout, braided nylon fishing line, 27-pound test or more so that it won't rip through the pages, and thread 3 inches of it through the eye of a needle. You'll be "sewing" with a single strand of thread, so twist the 3-inch segment around the longer segment to keep it from pulling through the needle's eye.
3. Hold the book face up, and thread the line down through the top hole, up through the second hole, down through the third hole, and so on, leaving at least 6 inches of line hanging out of the top hole. When you get to the last hole, repeat the process, this time heading for the top of the book.
4. When you come through the second hole from the top, both ends of the thread will be sticking out of adjacent holes on the front side of the book. Tie them together as tightly as you can using a square

FIGURE 3-1. A field guide drilled, sewn, and ready for taping.

knot. Snip off any excess thread, then melt the ends of the thread with a match or lighter to keep them from fraying.

5. Use 1½-inch cloth tape to cover your handsewn binding, and also run tape along the edges of the cover. Avoid nylon fiber tape, plastic tape, and rubber tape. They break down and get messy with age. Mystik cloth tape by Borden, Inc. is ideal.

A paperback protected in this way will last until reading wears away the print.

WRITERS AND POETS

In a letter to Robert Hooker, Isaac Newton (1642–1727), the most famous scientist/mathematician of his day, wrote, "If I have seen further (than you and Descartes) it is by standing upon the shoulders of giants." Scientists from that day to this have used the quote to acknowledge their dependence on work done by others; no scientist starts from scratch. Unfortunately, many nature appreciators do. Although we often take advantage of work done by natural scientists, we tend to overlook the wisdom left behind by writers and poets, who are often more directly concerned with nature appreciation.

When appreciating a particular object or event, each of us could save time and enhance the quality of his or her experience by incorporating insights gleaned from a wide variety of writers and poets. Who, for example, is so rich in insight and imagination that he or she can afford to face April without the help of the following three observations?

> _At its best, April is the tenderest_
> _of tender salads made crisp by ice or snow water._

John Burroughs
"April"
The Writings of John Burroughs,
Vol. III. Boston:
Houghton Mifflin Co., 1904

> _April is the cruellest month, breeding_
> _Lilacs out of the dead land, mixing_
> _Memory and desire, stirring_
> _Dull roots with spring rain._

T. S. Eliot
"The Waste Land"
T. S. Eliot Collected Poems
New York: Harcourt, Brace
and World, Inc., 1970

> _The sun was warm but the wind was chill._
> _You know how it is with an April day_
> _When the sun is out and the wind is still,_
> _You're one month on in the middle of May._
> _But if you so much as dare to speak,_
> _A cloud comes over the sunlit arch,_
> _A wind comes off a frozen peak,_
> _And you're two months back in the middle of March._

Robert Frost
"Two Tramps in Mud Time"
The Poetry of Robert Frost
New York: Holt, Rinehart
and Winston, 1969

Some woodsy types may find it hard to accept, but like science, nature appreciation is a cultural phenomenon. Woodchucks don't gaze at the moon.

Of course, Thoreau's writings are packed with specific observations and techniques. In *Walden*, for example, he refers to a technique for appreciating ponds and lakes that might be called the "cosmic compass needle." Take a rowboat, or better yet a canoe, and paddle to the largest stretch of open water on a lake. Then stow your paddle and lie back on the top of the canoe, head on the stern deck, seat on a thwart or elevated stern seat, arms and legs draped along the gunnels, fingers and toes dangling in the water. Now relinquish control to the cosmic winds and watch the round sky dance to the tune of distant waves lapping unseen shores.

Although you may have invented on your own the cosmic compass needle and some of the other specific techniques that Thoreau describes, his comments on them are still worth reading. They'll enable you to connect your experiences with the experiences of another person in another time. That's connection making of the first order.

Take advantage of John Muir as well. His descriptions make rocks and waterfalls come alive, and he is a good source of adventurous appreciating techniques. For example, in "Wind-Storm in the Forest" (Muir, John. *The Mountains of California*. New York: The Century Co., 1898), Muir describes a technique for appreciating gales:

> After cautiously casting about, I made a choice of the tallest of a group of Douglas Spruces [Douglas firs] that were growing close together like a tuft of grass, no one of which seemed likely to fall unless all the rest fell with it. Though comparatively young, they were about 100 feet high, and their lithe, brushy tops were rocking and swirling in wild ecstasy. Being accustomed to climb trees in making my botanical studies, I experienced no difficulty in reaching the top of this one, and never before did I enjoy so noble an exhilaration of motion. The slender tops fairly flapped and swished in the passionate torrent, bending and swirling backward and forward, round and round, tracing indescribable combinations of vertical and horizontal curves, while I clung with muscles firm braced, like a bobolink on a reed.

There are no Douglas firs in the Eastern forests, but a tall white pine might serve as well. And if the pine should prove less limber than the fir? That would be a consummatory experience indeed!

The writings of the following three authors will help you set the literary foundation of your qualitative natural history library:

HENRY DAVID THOREAU (1817–1862), *The Journal of Henry David Thoreau.* Vols. I–XIV. Edited by Bradford Torrey and Francis H. Allen. Boston: Houghton Mifflin Co., 1906; reprint edition, New York: Dover Publications, Inc., 1962.

———— *The Writings of Henry David Thoreau.* Vols. I–VI. Walden Edition. Boston: Houghton Mifflin Co., 1906; reprint edition, New York: AMS Press, Inc., 1968.

Princeton University Press is in the process of publishing a new and definitive edition of Thoreau's writings. *A Week on the Concord and Merrimack Rivers, Walden,* and several other volumes are already available.

JOHN MUIR (1838–1914), *The Writings of John Muir.* Vols. I–X. Sierra Edition. Boston: Houghton Mifflin Co., 1917. Reprints of this set are not available, and original sets are expensive and hard to find. But you can purchase much of what the set contains, and more, in individual paperbacks from a number of publishers, including the University of Wisconsin Press and the Houghton Mifflin Co.

JOHN BURROUGHS (1837–1921), *The Writings of John Burroughs.* Vols. I–XXIII. Riverby Edition. Boston: Houghton Mifflin Co., 1904; reprint edition, New York: Russell and Russell, 1968.

Leave room for the other literary naturalists, and some, too, for Dickinson, Welty, Frost, Eiseley, Wordsworth, Macleish, and many other authors whose writings deserve at least as much space on your natural history shelves as do field guides.

NATURE LORE

With literary works anchoring one end of your library and field guides anchoring the other, you can fill the space between with books on nature lore, such as Palmer's *Fieldbook of Natural History* (New York: McGraw-Hill Book Co., 1975); Martin, Zim, and Nelson's *American Wildlife and Plants: A Guide to Wildlife Food*

Habits (New York: Dover Publications, Inc., 1951); and Gibbons's *Stalking the Wild Asparagus* (New York: David McKay Co., Inc., 1962).

Binoculars

Using binoculars solely for magnifying distant objects is like drinking fine wine solely for medicinal purposes. Binoculars can do much more; think of them as vehicles for jumping perceptual ruts. When the fields in your neighborhood begin looking a bit too tame, look at them through the wrong end of your binoculars. You'll be transported to the wide-open spaces of Montana. Hold them normally and focus on rippling water, and they'll serve as a kaleidoscope, or look up and let them carry you to the pristine galleries of white pine cones and tassels. They'll even transform nondescript brown birds into white-throated sparrows with bright yellow lores. Used imaginatively, binoculars provide fresh perspectives by making the familiar look strange. (Binoculars were not generally available in Thoreau's day, but in 1854 he purchased a "spy-glass" and from then on used it regularly.)

When choosing binoculars for nature appreciation, consider the features discussed below.

FIELD-OF-VIEW

Field-of-view refers to the diameter of the view a binocular provides at a given distance, and it is often expressed as yards (or meters) at 1000 yards (or meters). For example, a 7 × 35 binocular might have a field-of-view of 150 yards at 1000 yards. This means that if two posts were placed 150 yards apart in an open field, at a distance of 1000 yards you'd be able to see both posts and everything between them. On the other hand, if you were using a 7 × 35 binocular with a field-of-view of only 122 yards, at 1000 yards you wouldn't be able to see both posts at once. In general, a wide field-of-view is better than a narrow one, because it makes spotting objects through the binocular easier.

A binocular with a field-of-view of at least 125 yards at 1000 yards will prove to be adequate *if* you're able to obtain the full field-of-view. Find out if you can by looking through the binocular—with your glasses on if you usually wear them. If you see two overlapping circles in a sea of black—an image similar to the one shown on the screen when someone looks through a binocular on television—you're not getting the full field-of-view. If you are getting the full field-of-view, you'll see *one perfect circle* with a *narrow* black margin around it. That's the view binoculars are supposed to provide, but you won't get it with your glasses on unless you're using a binocular with *extended eye relief.*

EYE-RELIEF

Eye-relief is the distance from the *ocular,* or *eyepiece* (the lens closest to your eye when binoculars are in use), to the *exit pupil* (see below). It is usually given in millimeters, and it tells you how close your eyes have to be to the oculars in order to get the full field-of-view. An ordinary binocular has an eye-relief of from 9 to 10 mm, which is adequate if you don't wear glasses, but if you do, it isn't because the lenses of your glasses will prevent you from getting your eye that close to the oculars. So if you wear glasses now or if you plan to grow old, at which point you might have to wear them, binoculars with extended eye-relief are for you.

Extended eye-relief binoculars, or "B" models as some manufacturers call them, have an eye-relief of approximately 15 mm instead of the usual 9 to 10 mm (Figure 3-2). This means that even with your glasses on you can get your eyes close enough to the oculars to see the full field-of-view. Extended eye-relief binoculars come with rubber eyecups that can be folded down when glasses are worn and extended when glasses are not worn. Many ordinary binoculars, however, also come with fold-down or retractable eyecups, and some manufacturers claim that these eyecups will provide eyeglass wearers with a full field-of-view. They won't. In themselves, fold-down eyecups and retractable eyecups are not enough. If you wear glasses, disregard all claims that imply that a particular model is suited to eyeglass wearers. Instead, either look through the

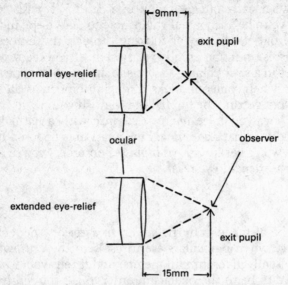

FIGURE 3-2. A comparison of normal eye-relief and extended eye-relief.

binocular to determine if the view is one, big, perfect circle, or ask for the eye-relief distance. If it's not 15 mm or more, the binocular won't provide the full field-of-view with your glasses on.

OBJECTIVE LENSES

The *objective lenses* are the large lenses at the wrong end of the binocular. The second figure in a binocular's identification number tells how large they are. For example, a 7 × 42 binocular has objective lenses that are 42 mm in diameter, and a 7 × 35 binocular has objective lenses that are 35 mm in diameter. Considerations such as power, weight, and lens quality aside, the bigger the objectives the better.

Essentially a binocular is a pair of light-gathering tubes. All usable light enters through the objective lenses, so given binoculars of the same power, the larger the diameter of the objective lenses the brighter the image you see. Pocket-size binoculars with objective lenses as small as 20 mm are available. They perform adequately in bright light, but they aren't worth carrying in the field, where you often have to work in deep shade, twilight, and other low-light situations. At dusk, 8 × 20s will make a distant object appear *darker* than it appears to the naked eye; 8 × 40s, on the other hand, will make the same object appear *brighter* than it appears to the naked eye. It's like having a low-power flashlight that doesn't disturb game. An 8 × 56 binocular will produce an even brighter image, but glass is heavy, and binoculars with objective lenses 50 mm and more in diameter are a chore to carry. For the naturalist, a 7- or 8-power binocular with 35 mm, 40 mm, or 42 mm objective lenses is a wise compromise between light-gathering ability and portability.

POWER

Power refers to the magnification a binocular provides. The first figure in a model's identification number tells you what it is. For example, a 7 × 42 binocular magnifies images seven times. In other words, it brings an object seven times closer to you, or more humbly, it brings you seven times closer to the object. Common sense, with an admixture of greed, would suggest that the higher the power the better the binocular, but it doesn't work that way in the field for two reasons. First, given the same objective lens size, the higher the power the darker the image; a 7 × 35 binocular will give you a brighter image in the shade than a 9 × 35 binocular. Second, higher powers, such as 9 and 10, make the motion that can't be avoided in hand-held binoculars more apparent, thus producing a jiggling image that can cause eyestrain. When asked if she didn't find her 10 × 40s hard on her eyes, a serious birder replied, "Sure, at the end of a long day I sometimes have a mild headache, but I identify a lot more warblers than I would with 8 × 40s." For certain applications, high power makes sense, but for qualitative natural history, 7- or 8-power binoculars are more than adequate.

EXIT PUPIL

An *exit pupil* is a point in space where light rays leaving an ocular converge to minimum diameter; that point is where your eye would normally be when using the binocular. (As was mentioned above, the exit pupil's distance from the ocular is called eye-relief.) Given lenses of equal quality, the larger the *diameter* of the exit pupil, the brighter the image you see when using a binocular, simply because more light can pass through a large hole than a small one. (You can see a binocular's exit pupils as two small circles of light, one on each ocular, by holding the binocular at arm's length toward a source of light.)

The diameter of an exit pupil is a function of the size of the objective lenses and the power of the binocular. In fact, you can calculate the diameter by dividing the size of the objective lenses by the power of the binocular. For example, a 7×35 binocular has an exit pupil 5 mm in diameter, while a 7×42 binocular has an exit pupil 6 mm in diameter and, consequently, a brighter image. As a general rule, the larger the objective lenses in relation to power, the larger the exit pupil and the brighter the image.

In addition to brighter images, binoculars with large exit pupils are also easier to use in situations where you can't hold them steady, as in a canoe or after a chase, again because it's easier to keep large holes aligned with your pupils than small ones. All things considered, large exit pupils are one of the most desirable features a binocular can have, so don't settle for one with exit pupils less than 5 mm in diameter.

FOCUSING

When using any binocular both barrels must be adjusted to suit your eyes. With *center focusing*, an initial adjustment is made for the right eye by turning either the right eyepiece or a *right eyepiece correction wheel.* After that, all focusing for both eyes is done by turning the *center focusing wheel.* With *individual eyepiece focusing,* every time you focus on an object, each eyepiece must be adjusted separately. This may not be a problem at sea, where binoculars are set on infinity and kept there for long periods, but in the woods, where objects are often viewed at close range and binoculars must be focused constantly, individual focusing is an eye-ripping hassle. To their credit, binoculars with individual focusing can be more tightly sealed against the elements than center-focusing binoculars, but unless you plan to submerge them often, quality center-focusing binoculars will take all the exposure you can.

Binoculars vary with regard to the minimum distance at which they can bring an object into focus. Some can focus on objects as close as 7 feet away; with others objects have to be at least 30 feet away. Since peering at nearby insects, mice, and fish is one of the great joys of using a binocular, when you have a choice between two models that are equal in all other respects, choose the one with the closest focusing, but check with the manufacturer before making your decision. Some models, such as the Zeiss 7 × 42B–GAT* Dialyte, can be modified by the manufacturer to focus closer than factory specifications indicate.

PORRO PRISM VERSUS ROOF PRISM

Porro prism binoculars are the most common. They're the ones with crooked barrels. _Roof prism_ binoculars, which are rapidly overtaking porro prisms in popularity, have straight barrels and are more compact and elegant. They also feel great in the hands, and since the space between objectives is less in roof prism binoculars, they're best for "going to Montana." The greater distance between objectives in porro prism binoculars does give slightly better depth perception, but this is usually not a difference that makes a difference.

BRANDS

Shoddy binoculars are an affront to the user and the environment. As Charles Bergman writes in _Audubon_ (see Recommended Reading), "By their very nature, binoculars are an intimate part of what is seen through them." Yet many binoculars are shoddy, or at best, second rate. In fact, if you wear corrective lenses or sunglasses, and you're interested in purchasing a quality binocular, there are only three readily available brands from which to choose: Leitz, Zeiss, and Nikon.

Ernst Leitz, Inc. Ernst Leitz, Inc., the company that makes Leica cameras, also makes the celebrated Trinovid binocular in twelve models; all have roof prisms and many have completely *internal focusing.* Ordinary binoculars have *external focusing*: as you focus them, the tubes in which the ocular lenses are mounted move up and down, actually increasing or decreasing the length of the binoculars. The length change is not a problem, but the corresponding change in the internal volume of the binoculars is, because it causes the binoculars to act as miniature bellows. As the volume inside binoculars changes, so does the internal pressure, and when the pressure inside the binoculars is less than the pressure outside, air with its burden of water vapor and dust can rush in and foul the lenses. Most manufacturers guard against this with rubber seals, but rubber seals break down with time and use. Leitz avoids the problem entirely by placing all moving lenses inside a rigid, weatherproof body.

Turn the central focusing wheel on a full-size Trinovid and look at the ocular end. You won't see anything move because the lenses do their moving inside the body. Even the right eyepiece corrects internally; this explains the distinctive second focusing wheel mounted on the bridge and the absence of a focusing mechanism on the right eyepiece.

Internal focusing does more than protect lenses from the elements; it makes for stronger, damage-resistant binoculars. Repairmen who work on external-focusing binoculars will tell you that one of the most common problems they face, other than worn seals, is bent external-focusing mechanisms, particularly the pin that slides in and out of the bridge as it moves the oculars up and down. If you drop a pair of Trinovids you may damage a lens, but you won't damage the internal focusing mechanism.

From the time they were introduced in 1967 until the mid-70s, when production was transferred from West Germany to Portugal, Leitz Trinovids were unquestionably the finest binoculars in the world. Leitz claims that today's Trinovids, which are made in Portugal, are every bit as good as the earlier German-made Trinovids. But the Portuguese-made Trinovids—or as Leitz prefers to call them, "German brand" Trinovids—are not assembled as carefully as the German-made Trinovids were, and at least one component of the Portuguese-made Trinovids is inferior to its erstwhile German-made counterpart.

For qualitative natural history, the 7 × 42B and 8 × 40B ("B"

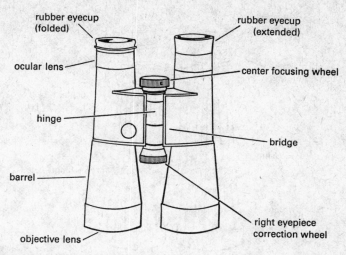

FIGURE 3-3. A 7 X 42B Leitz Trinovid binocular with completely internal focusing and roof prisms.

indicates extended eye-relief) models are the best in the line (Figure 3-3). The 7 × 42B jiggles less than the 8 × 40B, and its larger exit pupil makes it an ideal night glass, but the 8 × 40B provides a tad more reach, even if it is a bit harder to use in a canoe. Try both models, then decide which best fits *your* face, hands, and eyes.

Full-size Trinovids list for approximately $1000, but you can get them for half that from discount suppliers (see Appendix). Although they are not what they once were, Trinovids are still fine binoculars.

Carl Zeiss, Inc. Zeiss makes both porro and roof prism binoculars, but they don't make a completely internal-focusing binocular. Four of their Dialyte models, the 8 × 30B, 10 × 40BT*, and their rubber-armored counterparts, are Trinovid look alikes, but only their center focusing is internal. Their right eyepieces adjust externally and so move up and down. Still, these Dialytes are quality binoculars, easily in the same class as Leitz Trinovids, perhaps above them in optics, if a step below them in design. Unfortunately, for reasons discussed above, neither the 8 × 30B nor the 10 × 40BT* is well suited for qualitative natural history.

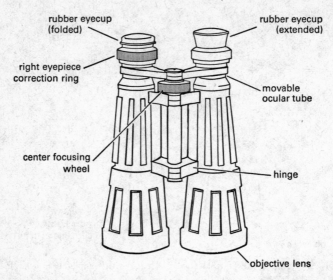

FIGURE 3-4. A 7 X 42B/GAT* Zeiss Dialyte binocular with external focusing and roof prisms.

The Zeiss Dialyte 7 × 42B/GAT* *is* ideally suited for qualitative natural history (Figure 3-4). Although it has external focusing, it does have roof prisms, rubber armor that won't peel off, rugged good looks, and the overall quality and finish one expects in a German-made glass. Zeiss thinks highly of it too, and they back it with a lifetime guarantee. The 7 × 42B/GAT* also has a newly developed lens coating, T*, which Zeiss claims transmits more light, making them even more effective under low-light conditions. They list for approximately $1000, but again, you can get them for about half that.

Nikon. Nikon binoculars are not in the same class as Leitz and Zeiss, nor do they cost as much. At present, the Nikon model best suited for nature appreciation is the 7 × 35E (Nikon uses "E" to indicate extended eye-relief), a porro prism, external-focusing glass with excellent optics. It lists for approximately $350, but you can get it for much less.

Other Brands. You can't speak of great binoculars without mentioning Bausch and Lomb, but you have to use the past tense. Their binoculars are now made in Japan, rather than on the shores of Lake Ontario in Rochester, New York. They may look pretty, but I've seen them fog internally in the field. There are several moderately priced German makes, such as Optolyth, which are worth examining if you have the opportunity to do so. The low-priced brands, of which there are many, are not only inexpensive, they're cheap.

PURCHASING

Before you buy a binocular, try the model you're interested in and several comparable models as well. Then order the one you prefer from one of the mail-order suppliers listed in the Appendix or check the advertisements in the back of photography magazines. You'll save a bundle.

Whichever binocular you choose, purchase a *hard* case for it if one is available. In addition, buy and use a rainguard, a small rubber or plastic hood that covers the oculars when the binocular is hung from your neck. It will keep dust, pollen, and raindrops off the oculars. When you do have to clean lenses, use a 100 percent cotton cloth that has been laundered many times.

If you decide to buy either a Leitz or Zeiss binocular, use it hard. These are good binoculars, not because of their well-known names or advertising, but because of their inherent quality. With good binoculars you *can* see and feel the difference.

Hand Lenses

A hand lens picks up where binoculars leave off. Unlike binoculars, however, you don't have to spend a great deal to get one, and you don't have to choose between brands of similar quality. There is a clear best: the Hastings Triplet made by Bausch and Lomb. It comes in 7-, 10-, 14-, and 20-power models. The greater the power, the smaller the Triplet, but even the largest will fit in an

English walnut shell. The 14-power Triplet is just about right for nature appreciation, and you can order one through a forestry supply house (see Appendix).

Each Triplet comes with a combination handle/cover. Many users string them on a stout cord or narrow ribbon and wear them around the neck, tucking the Triplet in a shirt pocket when it's not in use. When you do use a Triplet, hold it immediately before one eye or directly against an eyeglass lens, then move your head toward the object you wish to view or move the object toward your head until it comes into focus.

Conclusion

A New York banker was giving a tour of the city to an upstate entomologist. As they walked along a crowded street, the entomologist tapped the banker on the shoulder, pointed to a potted shrub, and said, "Listen, there's a field cricket singing in there." The banker was amazed that the entomologist had heard the cricket's song above the city's roar and complimented the scientist on his "good ears." A short time later, the banker stopped at a crack in the sidewalk and picked up a dime.

Thought Questions

1. You need a binocular to amplify your vision, but you don't need anything special to amplify your hearing. How's it done?

Hint: Watch a cat at rest as it listens to the sounds around it. You can't move your own ears like that, and besides, with any luck at all your ears are much smaller proportionately than a cat's. Still, you can use the cat's method by cupping your hands behind your ears and pointing them toward the source of sound. Try it right now with your radio's volume set very low.

2. Look at an object 15 or 20 feet away from you through a hand lens. (You'll have to hold the hand lens away from your eye to bring the object into focus.) Note that the object appears upside down and inverted right to left. All convex lenses do that. Why, then, don't you see the world upside down and inverted right to left when you look through your binocular?

Hint: Binoculars have more than magnifying lenses inside of them. They also contain prisms that flip images right side up and revert them left to right. Prisms also increase the distance light travels within a binocular, because light is deflected back and forth within the prisms and must travel a crooked path through the barrels rather than a straight one. This increase in focal length means that high magnification can be obtained without a corresponding increase in the actual length of the binocular. By the way, the lenses in your eyes also turn images upside down, and that's the way images strike your retinas. But your brain, rather than a set of prisms, sets things right again, so you don't have to walk on the ceiling.

3. If you live in the Northeast, Thoreau's *Journals* may be of more use to you on a day-to-day basis than any of his other writings. Why?

Hint: Thoreau dated his journal entries, so after a day afield you can compare your notes with Thoreau's for the same date during the years from 1837 to 1861. These comparisons will add to your appreciation of creatures such as muskrats and snapping turtles as you discover how faithful these merry creeps have remained to their ancestral ways. You'll also learn that the "present moment" that Thoreau sought to enjoy is the same one that so often eludes you and me.

4. No natural habitat presents a greater threat to binoculars than an ocean beach. Why?

Hint: It's not the water, it's the stuff at the edge of it. If the great research universities worked for a thousand years, they couldn't come up with a greater threat to optical instruments than sand. It can cause problems for binocular hinges and focusing mechanisms, and it can permanently damage lenses. Even one grain nestled between a cleaning cloth and a lens means scratched glass.

5. A binocular can be an asset when doing qualitative natural history, but a camera—unless used sparingly and with circumspection—is apt to be a liability. Why?

Hint: Binoculars are in harmony with the go-light philosophy and be-here-now attitude that characterize qualitative natural history; they're self-contained, simple to operate, and they literally focus attention on the here and now. Cameras, on the other hand, draw gadgets to them, they are relatively complex instruments to operate, and they take your attention away from the here and now to a future of prints and slides. For example, instead of an end to be enjoyed in *it*self, a colorful mushroom can easily be seen as a means to an arresting print. When that happens, present joys are sullied by future concerns. Moreover, taking pictures is still a *taking*, and the spirit of unity one hopes to achieve in the woods is lost as images of sunsets and wildflowers are reduced to mere possession.

Cameras do have a place in qualitative natural history: they're excellent record makers. In most instances, however, it's better to make a sketch than to take a picture. If you must have something between you and the woods, binoculars are bad enough.

Recommended Reading

BERGMAN, CHARLES A. "The Glass of Fashion." *Audubon*, November 1981, pp. 74–80. Bergman discusses the developmental history of binoculars, explains how they work, and offers specific suggestions for choosing a make and model. Worth reading even if you already own a binocular.

"Binoculars." *Consumer Reports*, March 1980, pp. 196–203. If you're thinking about buying a moderately priced binocular, this article may prove useful. Of the forty-seven models rated, about half are compacts, which are worse than useless for nature appreciation; the rest are 7 × 35s. No full-size models by Leitz or Zeiss were tested. Before you decide anything based on this article, remember that the thing an inexpensive binocular does best is gather dust in the closet.

BROOKS, PAUL. *Speaking for Nature.* Boston: Houghton Mifflin Co., 1980. An excellent introduction to the American nature appreciators who came after Thoreau. Packed with well-chosen quotes and thoughtful commentary. It's a good book to have because it will lead you to many more.

CHAPTER FOUR
The Way Home

---

*The man who walks to solve an internal problem on his
mind, or to daydream, is going to learn nothing about
natural navigation.*

Harold Gatty
Nature Is Your Guide, 1958

Relying on a map and compass to find your way in the woods is like swimming with waterwings on; both activities will keep you from developing basic skills. With a map and compass, navigating is reduced to a mechanical exercise in which your attention must be divided among the woods, a piece of paper, and a magnet. But without a map and compass, all of your attention can and must be focused on the woods.

A *natural system of navigation*—one based on using your senses and memory, rather than artificial aids—is described in the first part of this chapter. It will enable you to walk into and out of the woods on your own. The remainder of the chapter contains directions for using maps and a compass to perform more sophisticated maneuvers, such as reconnoitering a new area in a minimum amount of time and finding your way to a predetermined spot on a map.

The Home-Center System

The *home-center system* is used so widely that most of us don't have a name for it. It consists of orienting yourself to a fixed starting point, or *home center*, and defining any position you take thereafter in terms of that point. The telling question is, "Where's home center?" and it's answered by maintaining a *mnemonic* (of the memory) thread with your starting point as you move away from it. Then, wherever a walk takes you, you can find your way back to your starting point—be it a house, a campsite, or car—by following the mnemonic thread in reverse.

Of course, you're not committed to retracing your steps each time you want to return to your starting point. If you've maintained a taut thread, you can construct a mental map of the area and cut a beeline to home. In other words, at each point along your path you should be able to point directly to your home center. This is the same technique you've used to enter a shopping mall through one

FIGURE 4-1. The home-center system and the self-center system of navigation. At any point along the walk the hiker using the home-center system can point to "home," be it a house, campsite, or car. (Based on an illustration in *Nature Is Your Guide* by Harold Gatty.)

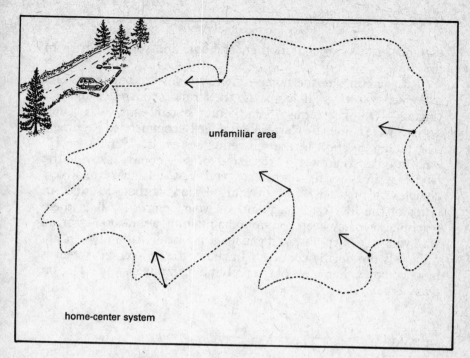

unfamiliar area

home-center system

unfamiliar area

self-center system

entrance, leave through another, and still find your way back to the car.

If you compare the home-center system to the more abstract *self-center system*, you'll appreciate the former's concrete simplicity (Figure 4-1). (The terms "home-center system" and "self-center system" were coined by Harold Gatty; see Recommended Reading.) The telling question in the self-center system is, "Where am I?" And in order to answer it, you have to use a compass, divide the landscape into north, south, east, and west, and make relatively complex calculations. Each of your positions is then described in terms of the four cardinal points on your compass. All of these machinations may keep you from maintaining a mnemonic thread with your starting point, so if you make a miscalculation, you're apt to be left thoroughly confused. In short, the self-center system is more complex than most of the pathfinding problems you'll face on a day hike.

SPINNING THE THREAD

The Lay of the Land. Hills, rivers, vegetation types, and cultural features are not randomly strewn over the landscape. Each piece of land has a distinctive *lay*, or *grain*, to it, and as a natural navigator you have to be aware of it. Then, like an orb-weaving spider, you can anchor your thread to pieces of the terrain that will hold it securely.

Prepare to spin your thread before you enter the woods by observing the lay of the land as you drive to your starting point. Are there any prominent mountains or hills in the area? Which way do the major valleys run? Where does the sun rise and set? Are there lakes or rivers in the area that the small streams in the woods will be heading for? Is there a highway nearby whose traffic sounds can be counted on as a reference point? Are the trees in the area bent by a prevailing wind? These sorts of questions will enable you to set the broad outlines of your mental map. In some situations, it's helpful to ask them from the roof of your car or from some other high point just before entering the woods.

Looking Back. The New Testament injunction against looking back may get you to heaven, but it won't get you back to the car, so look back often as you walk away from your starting point. This is the view you'll be faced with on your return, and anything you can do to fix it in your mind at the outset will be of help later on.

Keeping Track. When spinning a thread it's important to have an accurate idea of the direction your course is taking as you move away from the starting point. If, for example, you assume you've been walking directly away from the starting point, when in fact you've been veering to the right, your mental map will be misleading. Two rules of thumb will help you monitor the direction of your course: (1) most individuals consistently favor one side or the other when going around obstructions; the majority go to the right, (2) like the liquid of which we are chiefly composed, most of us follow the path of least resistance.

Rule 1 is especially important when walking over terrain that has lots of obstructions. As you cruise through a forest, for example, trees may cause you to make tens of left-or-right decisions. If you make these decisions unconsciously, you're apt to go to the same side of every tree that gets in your way. In time, this will cause you to veer drastically to one side, even though you may think you're walking a straight line. So either keep track of your deviation and correct for it occasionally, or avoid deviating in the first place by alternating between left and right decisions as you walk along.

Rule 2 is important when you're facing a constant source of resistance or irritation. For example, if you're being buffeted by a strong wind from your left, chances are you'll veer to the right. Similarly, if you're traversing a slope, your natural tendency will be to give in to gravity and veer downslope. Again, when you find yourself in these situations, you can either make periodic course corrections, or you can remain conscious of the forces working against you and constantly resist them. In situations where you're not particularly concerned with walking a straight line, you need not correct or resist, but in order to spin an accurate thread you must at least be aware of your direction.

Distance. It's often helpful to know how far you've walked in one direction, but many of us have difficulty estimating linear distances, so it's best to measure distance in terms of time. Think of yourself as having walked in a particular direction for two hours, rather than for 4 miles. When using time to find your way home, make allowances for changes in the terrain and in your levels of energy and interest, each of which can affect your speed. It takes longer to walk up a hill than down one; a tired hiker walks slower than a rested one; and as boredom increases, speed increases.

MODIFICATIONS

You don't have to be a purist when using the home-center system. You'll find it easier to make a mental map of an area if you study a paper map of it beforehand, and when you're on the trail, you might even sneak a look at your compass now and then. The trick is to use your maps and compass as occasional aids, rather than as the sole means of your pathfinding ability.

Topographic Maps

Ask a hiker to describe a place and you'll hear such words as "flat," "hilly," and "mountainous." Yet most road maps don't indicate these vertical features in any detail, so road maps are usually not of much use on a hike. In the woods you need a map that shows the nature of the terrain as well as the roads. *Topographic maps* (from the Greek words *topos*, meaning "place," and *graphein*, meaning "to write") do just that.

WHERE TO BUY TOPOGRAPHIC MAPS

In the United States, topographic maps are produced by the United States Geological Survey, a division of the Department of the Interior. You can buy topos at some outdoor stores, but it's often easier and cheaper to get the maps you want by dealing directly with the source. Start by writing to:

National Cartographic Information Center
507 National Center
Reston, Virginia 22092.

Request the following three items: (1) the booklet entitled *Topographic Maps*, (2) the *Index to Topographic Maps* for your state and any other state you're interested in, and (3) a *Map Order Form* for each state index you request. All of these items are free for the asking.

Topographic Maps contains a brief description of how topos are made, an explanation of how to read them, and a complete *legend* listing the symbols used on the maps. A state index consists of a large map of a state or states that has been divided into rectangles, or *quadrangles*, each of which bears the name of the topographic map that represents it. (Topographic maps are often named after the most distinctive physical or cultural feature in the quadrangle they represent.) All the quadrangles in a state are listed alphabetically on the order form for that state. All you have to do is put a check beside the name of each map you wish to order. Topos of the *woodland series*, the maps you'll want for hiking, sell for under $2 each.

Canadian topographic maps and information concerning them can be obtained by writing to:

Canada Map Office
Department of Energy, Mines and Resources
615 Booth Street
Ottawa, Ontario K1A 0E9.

HOW TO READ TOPOGRAPHIC MAPS

Date. Start with a topographic map that covers an area you're familiar with. Spread it before you. Then, as Dr. William Harlow recommends in *Ways of the Woods* (see Recommended Reading, Chapter 2), look for three things: "the date, the Date, and the DATE." You'll find the date your map was first printed on the left side of the lower margin and the date it was last field checked on the right side under the quadrangle's name. The field check date is most important, because like it or not, things change. If your map is an old one, it won't show houses, roads, and other additions that have appeared since it was printed, but it may show houses and barns that have long since gone down.

Scale. Check the *scale* next; it's in the center of the lower margin. Many of the newer maps have a scale of 1:24000. That means that 1 inch on the map represents 24,000 inches, or 2000 feet in the field. Some maps, particularly older ones that cover relatively unsettled areas, are drawn to a scale of 1:62500, meaning that 1 inch on the map represents 5,208.3 feet, or approximately 1 mile. A scale of 1:24000 is said to be a larger scale than a scale of 1:62500, because it shows greater detail. Contiguous maps are generally drawn to the same scale, so you can piece them together by folding their margins under. You'll see topographic maps with smaller scales (for example, 1:250,000) offered for sale on state indexes, but the large-scale, or woodland series maps, are best for field use.

Contour Lines. The wavy, and sometimes concentric, brown lines you see all over the map are *contour lines*. They represent hills, valleys, and other vertical features of the terrain (Figure 4-2). Each contour line passes through points that are the same elevation above sea level. In a sense, the shoreline of a pond is a natural contour line and so is a bathtub ring. The *contour interval,* or elevation between lines, is given just below the scale in the center of the lower margin. It may vary from map to map, but in general, the steeper the terrain the greater the contour interval. On maps of the Northeast, 10- and 20-foot intervals are common.

Whatever the interval, widely spaced contour lines indicate relatively flat or gently sloping terrain, and contour lines drawn close together indicate steep going. Note that some contour lines, every fourth or fifth depending on the contour interval, are darker and wider than the others. These are called *index contour lines,* and the lighter lines between them are called *intermediate contour lines.* Trace along an index contour and you'll soon come to a break in the line in which its elevation is printed.

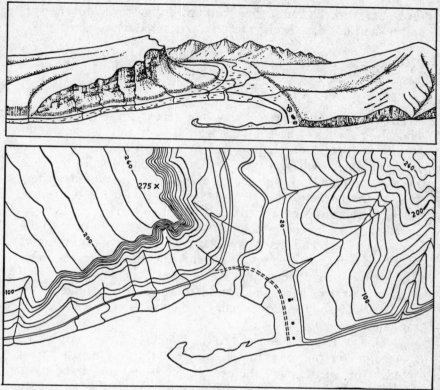

FIGURE 4-2. A bird's-eye view of a river valley and the same river valley as it might be represented on a topographic map. (Based on an illustration in *Topographic Maps* by the U.S. Geological Survey.)

On some maps you may come across contour lines that form closed figures with evenly spaced ticks on their inside edges. These are called *depression contours,* and that's just what they represent. Depression contours are of interest to naturalists because they sometimes indicate the presence of bogs (Chapter 9).

In addition to contour lines, over 100 other lines, symbols, colors, and shadings are used to represent features from mine shafts to marshes. This kind of detail makes for interesting reading. In fact, just as there are broken-down, old English professors who read dictionaries for pleasure, there are broken-down old hikers who spend their last days reading faded topographic maps.

USING A TOPOGRAPHIC MAP WITHOUT A COMPASS

Begin by taking the map to a spot that appears on it—a spot with enough character to be easily recognized both on the map and in the field. A point on a pond, the intersection of two roads, or a large building, such as a barn or country church, will do. Once there, locate your position on the map. Then use prominent features of the landscape to orient the map so that it lies before you just as the terrain does. When *visually orienting* a map to the terrain in this way, it sometimes helps to pretend that you're built to the scale of the map and that you're standing on the spot on the map that represents the spot you're actually standing on in the field. Then if you see a pond to your right on the map, you should see a pond to your right in the field, and if there is a barn behind you on the map, when you look over your shoulder you should see a barn in the field.

Once the map is oriented to the landscape, you can use both to reconnoiter the area. Simply pick out the features that most interest you on the map, then use the map and the landscape to guide yourself to them. This is a quick way to familiarize yourself with new areas. If you get confused, walk to the nearest distinctive feature in the field, locate it on your map, then orient the map and yourself once again.

Map and Compass

Map and compass go together like pizza and beer—you get more out of each one when the other is present—particularly if you use an *Orienteering compass*: a compass with a *revolving dial, orienting arrow,* and *sighting device* of some kind mounted on a clear plastic rectangle, or *base plate.* Several companies make them, but those made by Silva (distributed in the United States by Johnson Camping

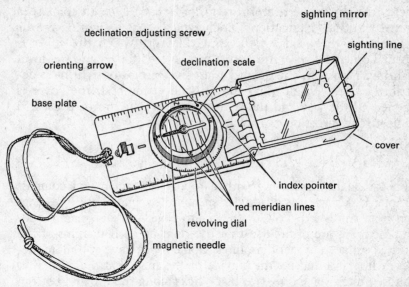

FIGURE 4-3. Silva Ranger Type 15 compass with parts labeled. The cover is open, and the compass is ready to use at waist level.

Inc., of Binghamton, N.Y.) are the originals, and they still set the standard of excellence.

Even the least expensive Silva Orienteering compass will get you from here to there, but it's worth the extra cost to purchase one of the Silva Ranger Type 15 compasses graduated from 0° to 360°, either the standard Type 15 or the Type 15CL, which has a built-in clinometer (Figure 4-3). You'll find the 0° to 360° graduations, where north is 0° or 360°, east is 90°, south is 180°, and west is 270°, less confusing than _quadrant graduations_, where north is 0°N, east is 90°E, south is 0°S, and west is 90°W. Each Type 15 has a built-in _declination adjustment_, which makes it easier to use than compasses without this feature, and each comes with an instruction manual that explains how to use it. Foresters, geologists, and several armies use the Type 15, so it may be all the compass you'll ever need.

With minor modifications the following directions will work for any Orienteering compass with a built-in declination adjustment, but they are written in terms of Ranger Type 15 compasses with 0° to 360° graduations. Each type 15 has a sighting mirror attached to the inside of the hinged cover. When the cover is opened only part way, the mirror can be used for precise eye-level sighting. However, the quicker *waist-level method* of sighting is described below. When using the waist-level method, the cover is opened all the way and the sighting line on the mirror is used to indicate the direction of travel.

NAVIGATING WITH MAP AND COMPASS

You can make navigating with a topographic map and compass simpler by drawing additional *meridian lines,* imaginary lines that run from the North Pole to the South Pole, on your map. Topographic maps are printed so that the right and left margins of the printed surface are meridian lines. Some topos have two more meridian lines printed on the surface of the map that divide it into thirds. Others have only two black ticks along the top and bottom margins, which can be connected to produce two meridian lines. Meridian lines and ticks are numbered in degrees, minutes, and/or seconds of *longitude* (for example, 76°45′; 42′30″; 40′; 76°37′30″). Longitude is measured west from the 0°0′0″ line, the *prime meridian,* which passes through Greenwich, England. (The top and bottom margins of the printed surface are *latitude lines,* and there are two latitude ticks along each side margin of the printed surface. Latitude lines and ticks are also numbered. The four points where longitude and latitude lines intersect on the surface of your map are indicated by black cross marks. You can use these cross marks to determine your approximate longitude and latitude.)

Whether your map has two or four meridian lines, you'll need more for easy navigating, so use a pencil (pencil lines won't run when wet) to draw a set of vertical lines spaced 1½ inches apart and parallel to the left and right margins. (Some find that lines two or more inches apart work as well. You'll be able to decide for yourself after you've done some navigating.)

You're right if you're thinking that neither meridian lines nor the left and right margins of your topographic map are parallel. Meridian lines meet at the poles, so the margins are a bit closer together at the top of your map than at the bottom. But the error you'll incur by drawing your meridian lines parallel is so small as to make no practical difference when day hiking.

Once the lines are drawn, cover the map with contact paper or coat it with one of the liquid sealants made especially for waterproofing maps. Then fold the map so that it will fit inside a sandwich-size zip-lock bag, and it's ready for field use. If you fold the map with the printed surface on the outside, you'll be able to read sections of it through the plastic bag. You can save space by cutting off the side margins, but if you do, copy the names of the contiguous quadrangles and other information printed in the margins onto the back of the map.

ADJUSTING YOUR COMPASS FOR DECLINATION

Because the meridian lines on your map point to the North Pole, which is also called _true north_ and _geographic north_, in a sense your map also points to true north. Unfortunately, the magnetic needle on your compass doesn't; it points to _magnetic north_, the spot in the Northern Hemisphere where the magnetic lines of force surrounding the earth converge. Magnetic north is presently situated over 1000 miles to the south of the North Pole and somewhere to the west of Hudson Bay. This means that in eastern North America your compass needle points west of true north, and in western North America your compass needle points east of true north.

At a given location, the difference between true north and magnetic north (the direction your compass points) is called _declination_, and it is measured in degrees west or east of true north. The easiest way to allow for declination—that is, the easiest way to bring your map and compass into harmony—is to use the declination adjustment on your compass. But in order to do so, you have to know what the declination is where you are.

The declination in an area is indicated on the left side of the lower margin of the corresponding topographic map. On older maps you'll see an angle formed by two lines labeled APPROXIMATE MEAN DECLINATION 19—. On newer maps you'll see three lines labeled UTM GRID AND 19— MAGNETIC DECLINA-

TION AT CENTER OF SHEET. In both cases, one of the lines in the *declination diagram* points to the North Pole, or true north. On older maps that line is labeled TRUE NORTH, on newer maps it's designated with a black star.

Either to the left (west) or right (east) of the true-north line (to the west in the East, and to the east in the West), you'll see a line with either an arrowhead or a barb at its tip; it points to magnetic north. The difference between the two lines, measured in degrees of declination, is printed close by. There are points on the continent where true north and magnetic north align. These points are located along an irregular line called the *agonic line* (meaning "no angle"), which presently passes through Florida, Tennessee, Illinois, and Ontario. If you're situated on or near the agonic line, the declination is 0° and no declination adjustment is required. Adjustment is required if you're located either east or west of the agonic line. In general, the farther you get from the agonic line, the greater the declination. Declination in North Carolina, for example, runs from approximately 2° to 6° west, while in Maine it runs from approximately 18° to 20° west.

To adjust your compass for declination (assuming it's a Silva Ranger Type 15), first find the declination in the area in which you'll be using it by checking the declination diagram on the appropriate topographic map. If it's a westerly declination, as it will be in the East, turn the declination adjustment screw, which is located on the compass dial, clockwise until the *orienting arrow* at the bottom of the compass housing points to the number on the western half of the *declination scale* that corresponds to the degree of declination indicated in the declination diagram. That's it; as long as you remain in the same area you can forget about declination.

GENERAL PRECAUTIONS

Now that you have drawn meridian lines on your topographic map and adjusted your compass for declination, you're ready to step into the field and navigate. When you do, keep the following in mind for the best results:

1. When you go to a new area, reset the declination on your compass for that area.

2. Magnetic north drifts west a bit each year, so the declination in a given locality changes a bit each year as well. Because this yearly change in declination is small, the declination given on your map will probably be accurate enough for hiking purposes, *if* your map has been field checked within the past ten to fifteen years. If your map is older than that, you may want to get a more current declination. You can do so by calling a local surveyor or by writing to:

   U.S. Department of Commerce
   Coast and Geodetic Survey
   Distribution Division C44
   Washington, D.C. 20235.

   For 50 cents they'll send you Publication Number 3077, the "Isogonic Chart of the United States," which contains current declinations for all states.

3. When using your compass, keep objects made of iron, steel, and nickel away from it; otherwise, the magnetic needle will point to them rather than to magnetic north. Some electronic gadgets, including certain cameras, may have a similar effect.

4. Hold your compass level when taking a reading so the magnetic needle can swing freely.

TAKING A BEARING FROM A MAP

Assume that you've spotted a small but interesting looking pond on a topographic map, and that you'd like to hike to it. As you study the map, you notice that there are no trails or roads leading to the pond—oh, fond fantasy!—and that it is surrounded by heavily wooded (green shading on the topo), relatively flat, homogeneous terrain. Because you won't be able to see far ahead once you're in the woods, and because there are no landmarks to see anyway, you realize that finding your way to the pond with the aid of the map alone will be problematic at best. Here's where your Orienteering compass, *adjusted for the area's declination*, comes in handy. Using it and a topographic map you can obtain a *bearing*, or a direction in compass degrees, to the pond.

First, orient the topo to the landscape. Although you don't have to do this, it may stay confusion later on. Here's a quick way to orient a map using a compass:

1. Unfold the map and place it on a flat piece of ground.
2. Open the cover of your Ranger Type 15 until it lies on the same plane as the base plate. Set the compass dial at 0°, or 360°, by aligning the 360° graduation on the dial with the *index pointer* on the base plate. Then place the compass on the map with its cover toward the top of the map, and align one edge of the base plate with either a meridian line or the true north line in the declination diagram. (The easiest way to do this is by bringing one edge of the base plate into contact with the line you have chosen.)
3. Now "weld" the compass to the map, and turn the map until the magnetic needle lies directly over the black *orienting arrow,* with the red end of the magnetic needle and the head of the orienting arrow together.

When these conditions are met, the features on the map will be oriented to the features in the landscape that they represent. Check this visually to be sure that you haven't made an error.

Next, take the compass and position the right (or left) edge of the base plate so that it touches both the spot where you are located and the spot where you want to go. If these two points are separated by a distance greater than the length of the base plate, connect them with a straight edge and place the base plate against it. Whichever method you use, position the compass on the map so that the open cover lies toward your goal.

Now, hold the compass in position on the map and turn the dial until the red meridian lines inside the housing are parallel with the meridian lines you drew on the map. As you turn the dial, keep the letter "N" on the dial toward the top of the map. (Note that *if* you have kept the map oriented to the landscape, when the two sets of meridian lines are parallel, the magnetic needle will lie directly over the orienting arrow. However, even if the map is not oriented to the landscape and the needle and arrow do not align, as long as the two sets of meridian lines are parallel, this system will work.)

Your bearing is now set, and you can find out what it is by reading the degree graduation on the compass dial indicated by the index pointer. If we assume that the pond is directly west of your position, the bearing indicated will be 270°.

FOLLOWING A BEARING

Now that your compass is set for the bearing you wish to follow, the next step is to transfer that bearing to the country you'll be walking through. Cradle the opened compass in one hand and hold it waist high in front of you, with the base plate toward you and the cover away from you. Make sure the compass is level, and don't move that dial. (This position is at least as picturesque as the one far-sighted old men assume when they gaze at their pocket watches, so enjoy it, and if there is anyone else around, maintain it for awhile so they can enjoy it too.) Then turn in your tracks until the magnetic needle is perfectly aligned with the orienting arrow. The sighting line on the mirror now points directly to the pond.

Use your imagination to project an extension of the sighting line straight out into the woods; then pick a tree or other object that lies somewhere in the distance on that line. You can put the compass in your pocket as you walk toward the object, or *marker*, which you have selected, but don't change the setting on the compass. If the pond is between you and the marker, you'll walk right to it; however, in the heavy forest of our example, your marker is apt to be between you and the pond. In that case, when you reach the marker walk halfway around it, take out your compass, sight your original bearing once again, and pick another marker. Repeat this process until you reach the pond.

If "following a bearing" isn't romantic enough for you, you can refer to the process as *shooting an azimuth*. "Azimuth" comes from the Arabic *as sumut*, roughly meaning "the way," and it is sometimes used as a synonym for "bearing."

Compass Alone

Let's assume that you're relaxing on a slope overlooking an extensive woods, and in the distance you see the top of a large white pine that you'd like to visit. You know that once you descend the slope, you'll lose sight of the pine. What do you do? Again, take a bearing. Hold your compass at waist level in the standard manner, face the pine, and project an extension of the sighting line to it. Then, without moving the base plate, turn the dial of your compass until the magnetic needle and orienting arrow are aligned. Your bearing is set. Pick a marker and be on your way.

Conclusion

Navigating with a map and compass is intriguing, and you can do far more with them than what has been described above, but as a qualitative naturalist it's more important to be expert with eyes and ears than with map and compass. If you rely on the latter, you may never get lost, and that would be a loss. For as Thoreau observed in *Walden*:

> It is a surprising and memorable and, I may add, valuable experience to be lost in the woods. . . . We are constantly steering like pilots by certain well known beacons and headlands, though we are not conscious of it, and if we go beyond our usual course we still preserve the bearing of some neighbouring cape, and not till we are completely lost or turned around . . . do we appreciate the vastness and strangeness of nature. . . . In fact, not till we are lost do we begin to realize where we are, and the infinite extent of our relations.

The woods get smaller every year, but if you know what you're doing, you can still get lost in them.

Thought Questions

1. The European sailing ships that serviced the first North American settlements were equipped with relatively primitive navigational aids, and even a skilled captain couldn't sail directly to the settlement for which his ship was bound. Usually a ship would make landfall somewhere up or down the coast from its destination, but the captain couldn't be sure which, and so had to sail up and down the coast until he found it. This trial-and-error method was a risky and time-consuming process, so savvy captains employed a technique that caused them to miss their destinations by many miles at first landfall, but left them knowing exactly which way they had to sail in order to find them. You can use this same technique to find your car when coming out of the woods after a long hike. What is it?

Hint: The technique is called *deliberate error.* When a ship left Europe, the captain would set and hold a direct course for its destination. Then, as the ship neared the coast, the captain would drastically alter the course, either up or down the coast *away* from the settlement. By making a deliberate error of greater magnitude than the inherent error of his navigational aids, the captain could be sure of which way to sail after sighting the coast. Similarly, when you're coming out of the woods and you have only a rough idea of where your car is, make a deliberate error to one side of it, and when you hit the road it's on, you'll know which way to walk in order to find it.

2. Assume that you're following a bearing of 290° through a dense forest and deep in the woods a rock outcropping blocks your way. You can't climb over it, so you have to go around it. How can you do so without changing the bearing on your compass?

Hint: Your Ranger Type 15 compass is mounted on a rectangular base plate. When the compass is set and sighted on a bearing, the side edges of the base plate are parallel to that bearing, and the end edges of the base plate are at right angles to it. You can take advantage of this configuration to navigate easily past obstructions.

Face the obstruction and orient your compass (align the magnetic needle with the orienting arrow) without changing the 290° bearing. Then take a sighting toward the right (or left if the going is easier in that direction) along the rear edge of the base plate. You'll have to hold the compass at just below eye level and to one side of your face to do this. Pick out a marker, and walk toward it, *counting* your paces as you go, until you reach the right end of the obstruction. Now orient your compass again. Take a sighting along the original bearing, pick a marker, and walk toward it until you are just past the obstruction. Orient the compass once again, and this time sight to the left along the rear edge of the base plate, back toward the outcropping. Pick a marker and walk toward it the *same number of paces* you walked to the right of your original course. Orient your compass yet again. The outcropping is now behind you, and the sighting line on your compass points to your original bearing of 290°. Instead of saying you walked halfway around the outcropping, you could say you walked halfway "asquared" it. (Foresters refer to this procedure as "running an offset.")

3. Many first-rate compasses have fluid-filled housings; their magnetic needles spin around in a clear fluid rather than in a gas such as air. What's the advantage of this?

Hint: The magnetic needle in a first-rate compass is mounted on an almost friction-free bearing. Your Ranger Type 15, for example, has a sapphire jewel bearing. If its magnetic needle were surrounded by air, it would meet with so little resistance that it would take a long time to stop spinning, and once it did, it would jiggle constantly as you held it.

4. If you plot a 5-mile course on a topographic map and then follow it in the field precisely—without varying even an inch—you'll still end up walking over 5 miles. Why?

Hint: Although topos show vertical features, distances measured on them are horizontal.

5. You can tell which way a particular stream on a topographic map flows by looking at the contour lines that cross it. What do you look for?

Hint: Contour lines connect points of equal elevation, and streams run in valleys and troughs that are lower in elevation than the country on either side of them. In addition, elevation increases as one proceeds up a stream. Therefore, when a contour line is drawn across a stream, in order to maintain elevation it must be bent *up* as it cuts across the first side of the stream's valley or trough. And at the center of the stream it must be bent *down* again in order to maintain elevation. These bends in contour lines produce "arrowheads" that point upstream.

Recommended Reading

GATTY, HAROLD. *Nature Is Your Guide.* New York: E. P. Dutton & Co., Inc., 1958. This is *the* book on natural navigation. Much of it has to do with finding your way at sea and in distant lands, but the concepts the book is built around can be applied anywhere.

GEARY, DON. *Step In The Right Direction.* Harrisburg, Pennsylvania: Stackpole Books, 1980. A book for the nature appreciator who wants to learn more about using a map and compass. Easy to follow, and the author's approach is in keeping with the spirit of qualitative natural history.

KJELLSTROM, BJORN. *Be Expert With Map & Compass.* New York: Charles Scribner's Sons, 1976. If you do all the exercises in this book, you'll be an expert with map and compass. Practice materials are included.

TUAN, YI-FU. *Topophilia: A Study of Environmental Perception, Attitudes, and Values.* Englewood Cliffs, New Jersey: Prentice-Hall, Inc., 1974. "Topophilia," from the Greek *topos* meaning "place" and *philia* meaning "loving," is the author's neologism, and he uses it to refer to all of the affective ties people have with the environment. A bit academic, but it's pleasant reading, and it's packed with insights on the roles perceptions and attitudes play in forming bonds between people and places.

CHAPTER FIVE
Walking

In my afternoon walk I would fain forget all my morning occupations and my obligations to society. But it sometimes happens that I cannot easily shake off the village. The thought of some work will run in my head and I am not where my body is,—I am out of my senses. In my walks I would fain return to my senses.

Henry David Thoreau
"Walking"
Writings, Vol. 5, 1906

Practitioners in every discipline rely on specialized techniques to get their work done; scientists conduct experiments, archeologists excavate ancient sites, and qualitative naturalists take walks. When used in this way, walking is neither a form of exercise nor a means of locomotion. It's a gentle art that will put you in sympathy with a piece of land faster and more consistently than any other.

Some of the know-how you'll need to master the art of walking is presented below in the form of a first principle and assorted suggestions listed under the headings How, When, and Where. Despite the pedantic tone that a list of this sort necessarily takes on, it is offered only as an overview of what walking is all about. The suggestions it contains are not absolutes and they are not step-by-step instructions; walking is not that kind of an activity. Like the baking of apple pies, walking is an activity whose products are more a function of the walker's temperament than the recipe followed.

First Principle

Nothing recommends a walk more than good reasons for not taking it. Walk often.

How

SITTING

The number of miles you can walk in a day is unimportant; what counts is the number of hours you can sit still. When you're on the move, every motion advertises your presence, and each footfall hollers "Here I come!" Wood thrushes stop singing, white-tailed deer skulk off for heavy cover, and woodchucks retire to their burrows. Sit still for twenty minutes and the business of the woods will pick up and continue as usual. If you get fidgety, lie down. You can cover a lot of ground lying on a bed of hair-cap moss.

COMPANIONS

John Muir made many of his great treks alone, and it is said that Thoreau once refused an offer of company by replying that he had "no walks to waste." In fact, Thoreau often walked with a companion, particularly his friend Ellery Channing, but like most first-rate naturalists, he was aware that company can be a liability on a walk. The problem is that people can come between you and the woods. A small-talking chickadee is simply no match for a fast-talking friend, and the quiet goodwill of a grove of white pines is easily overwhelmed by a boisterous group of companions. Two or three friends who know what they are doing *may* be able to slip into the context of a woodland day and enjoy it together, but a party of more than three creates a new context, and the group replaces the woods as the phenomenon of interest.

Dogs on a walk are like people, but worse. Their enthusiasm and tail-wagging camaraderie make them centers of attention, they spook other animals, and they may bother other walkers. Tail-wagging and people-bothering excepted, the same is true of woods-walking cats. Granted, walking in the woods with a dog or cat is an instructive and satisfying experience in its own right. In terms of qualitative natural history, however, it is *generally* less productive than walking alone or with one or two human friends.

SEEKING

Just as the driver of a car who must pay attention to the road will see more on either side of it than passengers who are free to look wherever they choose, the individual who enters the woods looking for a particular thing will see more of everything. Carry a mental image of an uncommon plant or animal that might be found where you're hiking and look for it as you walk about. This will keep your senses keen, and if the species you're looking for is present, you'll probably spot it. In fact, if your image of the species is clear and your desire to see it is strong, you may be able to materialize it—at least it will sometimes seem that way. "Seek and ye shall find" is good advice in any context.

NOTEBOOK

Carry a field notebook and make a record of each of your walks. Record anything that interests you: How is the acorn crop this year? What are the gray squirrels feeding on? What wildflowers are in bloom? Include sketches when you can. They don't have to be perfect, just recognizable—to you. Notes and sketches will add to your walks in two ways. First, writing and sketching will slow you down. It's all too easy to dismiss a flowering bloodroot with a "Wow!" and then walk on, but if you stop to make a few notes and a sketch, you'll find that the shape of the leaf alone is worthy of prolonged contemplation. (While you're down there, dig up a section of the root, bruise it, and color a corner of a page with its sap. They don't call them bloodroots for nothing.) Second, notes and sketches will add a new dimension to your walks because written records make it possible to connect events separated by time. If your notebooks for the last three years indicate that each time you found wild ginseng it was growing close-by doll's eyes and blue cohosh on heavily wooded, north-facing slopes, then heavily wooded, north-facing slopes with doll's eyes and blue cohosh will come to mean the possibility of fabled ginseng. You'll find connection-making of this sort especially satisfying because it's a source of predictive power.

If you have to open your pack to get your notebook—you won't. So carry a notebook that fits comfortably in your shirt pocket. A 3 × 5 inch, side-opening memo book with forty narrow-ruled sheets stitched to a stiff paper cover works well. You can buy these memo books singly or in boxes of twenty-four at stationery stores. Ask for Memo Book 45-9852(809) by Vernon McMillan, Inc. (Figure 5-1). Some outfitters sell similar, but somewhat larger, notebooks with waterproof pages. These might be fine if you can afford them, although Thoreau, Muir, and Leopold made do with ordinary paper. Avoid notebooks with spiral bindings; they snag pockets. Any binding other than simple stitching is apt to be uncomfortable if you lean on it, and if you carry a notebook at all times, you'll lean on it. Don't be taken in by the little black beauties with hard, imitation leather covers. They're too heavy and will fall out of your pocket each time you bend over.

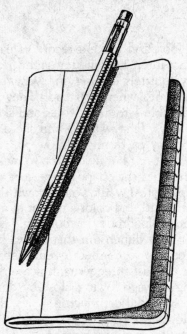

FIGURE 5-1. A field notebook and pencil.

Penciled field notes won't wash out or fade away when they get wet, and they are easy to make if you use a mechanical pencil with a pocket clip. Expensive mechanical pencils are usually heavy and their erasers are often hidden somewhere deep inside of them, but inexpensive models by Scripto and Pentel are lightweight and their erasers are brazenly displayed at one end.

Habituating yourself to carrying and using a notebook may take some doing, but once you're hooked, you won't enter the woods without one. Before long, your completed notebooks will occupy a place of honor on your natural history bookshelves, and you'll agree that jackknives and binoculars notwithstanding, a field notebook is a vade mecum second to none.

CACHE OR CARRY?

Keep it with you. Inexperienced walkers often make this simple mistake: Early in the walk they decide to *cache* (conceal on the trail or in the woods) an unneeded jacket or a newly found woodchuck skull, planning to retrieve it on the way back. Reasonable enough, except that "way leads on to way" in the woods, and the way you take in may not be the way you take out. New paths and new purposes often appear while you're on the trail, and a cache is a commitment that can keep you from taking advantage of them. Remain free and unattached on your walks.

COURTESY

Well over a century ago, Thoreau ("Walking," in *Writings*, Vol. 5, 1906) predicted that the day would come when "walking over the surface of God's earth shall be construed to mean trespassing on some gentleman's grounds." That day is here. The American (via the English) tradition of free trespass is slipping into oblivion. "Posted" and "No Trespassing" signs are everywhere. Much posting, however, is done to keep hunters out, so if you approach landowners courteously, many of them will give you permission to walk on their land. If any deny your request, shake the dust from your moccasins as testimony against them and walk on.

When you do find a place to walk, be mindful of the legitimate rights and needs of others. Park your car well away from houses and be careful not to block farm and logging roads. Walk along the unplanted edges of crop and hay fields. A shortcut taken through a field of alfalfa will leave a telltale trail of bent and unharvestable stems. When climbing over a barbed-wire fence, you may damage it; slip under the bottom strand on your back instead. Stay well away from farm buildings (even seemingly abandoned ones), farm animals, and farm equipment. You know you're only looking, but the owner doesn't. When possible, stay out of sight. It's highly unlikely that your figure in the landscape will add to the owner's view.

If you should encounter a landowner in the field, introduce

yourself and explain what you're doing. "Bird-watching" will satisfy most people, especially if your binoculars are prominently displayed on your chest. (If you tell someone that you're "methodologically applying Thoreauvian techniques in an attempt to derive satisfaction from natural objects and occurrences," you may be asked to leave.) Thank the obliging owner for allowing you to walk on his or her land and remember that an annual note of thanks will be appreciated, especially if it's tucked in a peck of apples.

When

TIMING

The natural day is like a loaf of bread: relatively bland in the middle and tasty at the ends. Birds, mammals, and colors generally come out when the sun is near the horizon, while comparatively little goes on in the middle of the day. Yet due to bad habits acquired in the work place, many of us plan our hikes so that we're in the woods from nine to five. This means that during most of the year we miss the two major events of the natural day, sunrise and sunset. So if you can't have the whole loaf, take one of the crusty ends. Leave the house before sunrise and plan to be back before noon or leave in mid-afternoon and plan to be back after dark.

NIGHT WALKS

Night walks are a good way to pick up a sunrise or sunset and they have other advantages as well. A crackerjack woodsman told me that he had given up walking during the day. "This area has gotten too crowded," he explained. "During the day my favorite places are often full of people, so now I go out only after dark. It's like turning the clock back thirty years." In addition to having the woods to yourself, you'll see things at night that you can't see during the day, including moon shadows, falling stars, and flying squirrels.

Unless you're doing something specific, such as mothing (Chapter 6), leave your flashlight in your pack. That way you'll experience what the night is justly famous for, and you'll have the opportunity to develop senses that are often overwhelmed by sight during the day. You may be surprised at how sensitive you become to sounds, odors, and slight variations in temperature as you skulk about the woods at night.

Although nowhere near as effective as an owl's or cat's, your eyes won't fail you entirely at night. In fact, on moonlit nights you'll be able to use your binoculars in certain situations. After you've been in the dark awhile, your eyes will undergo both chemical and physical changes that improve night vision. During the first fifteen minutes, your pupils dilate from their usual daytime diameter of from 3 to 4 millimeters to a nighttime maximum of from 7.5 to 8 millimeters. After forty-five minutes or so, the color sensitive cones on your retinas recede as light-sensitive rods come to the fore. At the same time, *rhodopsin*, a light-sensitive pigment sometimes called *visual purple*, saturates the rods, leaving your eyes at their nighttime best.

If you have to use a flashlight after you've acquired night vision, cover the lens with a red filter or a piece of red cellophane. You'll find the red light less shocking and so will the many nocturnal creatures who see red light as gray.

WEATHER AND SEASONS

They may talk about "bad weather" on the radio, but the term is misleading in the woods. Heavy weather brings out new aspects of familiar places. A vacant lot can appear wild and wooly in a dense fog. Moreover, some plants and animals are at their best in the rain; the great burdock sucks its belly in and stands at attention, and the red eft, the immature land form of the red-spotted newt, seems to come out of hiding. Heavy weather brings out good things in people too. As Liberty Hyde Bailey ("Wind and Weather," in *Wind and Weather*. New York: Charles Scribner's Sons, 1916) wrote:

> Passengers on the cosmic sea
> We know not whence nor whither,
> 'Tis happiness enough to be
> Complete with wind and weather.

When it rains, tuck Bailey's poem under your hat and head out.

The first person to appreciate fully the seasonal changes that take place around a typical Northeastern pond will probably be able to walk on its waters in July as well as January. The woods are constantly changing, and every spot offers at least 365 different walks a year. Hence John Burroughs' maxim, "To learn something new take the path you took yesterday."

Where

FINDING GOOD SPOTS

You can find places to walk on your own or someone else can tell you about them. In either case, topographic maps (Chapter 4) will prove useful.

When working on your own, look over the appropriate topos and watch for likely spots as you drive about. If a spot looks interesting on a map, drive out to it and follow the roads around it. If it still looks interesting, explore it on foot. Similarly, if you spot an area while you're driving, check it out on a topographic map. If it still appeals to you, go back and explore it. Don't overlook small areas and waste places.

Expert advice can save you a lot of time in the car, and the local chapter of the Audubon Society is one place to obtain it. Find out when their next field trip is and go along. If you like the spot, you can always go back to it on your own. More important, during the trip you're sure to meet people who know your area well, and they'll be able to tell you about other good spots.

Hiking clubs, biology and geology professors who teach field courses, and local guidebooks are other sources of expert advice. Don't forget hunters and fishermen; they know where the pheasant covers and secluded trout streams are. As a group they're generally a bit shy about giving their best spots away, but if you explain that you're not planning to hunt or fish, they may direct you to some fine areas. If you don't know any fishermen or hunters, the best places to meet them are the local sportsmen's club—try the bar first, then the trap range—and locally owned rod and gun shops. Talk with anyone you can find who enjoys the out-of-doors. Volunteer some information about your favorite spots and you'll find that one good spot leads to another. Of course, you'll want to display some moderation in this regard. The sportsman's age-old tradition of maintaining *secret spots* is not without value.

ACROSS LOTS

In unsettled areas trails and abandoned roads are often ideal for walking, but in settled areas they tend to be garbage-strewn ruts, so when you're attempting to come back to your senses, step off the trail and pick your way through the woods. Walk *across lots*. When walking a trail it's all too easy to maintain an aggressive workaday pace, but when walking across lots, briars and brush will slow you down and the process of setting your own course will keep your attention on the woods. Walking across lots does not necessarily mean making a beeline or bushwacking through heavy cover. Follow the path of least resistance; walk around obstacles. Your goal is to walk *in* the woods, not through them.

Deer trails are lessons in walking softly. Follow them when you can. Deer know the places where dogs and people don't go, and they know where to find the tastiest wild apples.

EDGES

Walk the edges. If you're in an area where a field meets a forest, for example, walk along the transition zone between the two. You'll see more species of plants and animals there than you'll see in either the forest or in the field alone. This seems reasonable enough, because in the transition zone you'll see species from both the forest and the field. But there's more to it than that. Transition-zone habitats are unlike the habitats around them, so they attract different species. Indigo buntings, for example, don't like dense forests or open fields, but they do like the edges where forests and fields meet. Whether a transition zone occurs between a forest and a field, a swamp and a lake, or a freshwater river and an ocean bay, it's called an *ecotone*. The increase in the number of species that an ecotone causes is called the *edge effect*.

In addition to transition zones between natural habitats, ecotones may also appear within a homogeneous habitat after drastic changes have occurred, such as those brought on by beaver dams, forest fires, and changes in land use. This explains the rich and rewarding walks that abandoned farmlands produce as pastures revert to forests. The brushy fields that spring up in the interim are similar to the natural ecotones that occur between forests and fields.

HIGHS AND LOWS

Seek out high and low places. You can get above mundane affairs by climbing to the top of a hill or a mountain; the long views will literally give you a new perspective on life. (Saints and seers don't climb mountains for the exercise.) In swamps and bogs the views are shorter, but far more intimate.

High slopes facing the southwest are ideal places to spend the day watching the sun rise, travel across the sky, and set. If the slope is steep enough, you can lie down, rest your head on your pack, and watch the landscape change colors without straining your neck. From a high perch you'll also be able to see interrelationships among landforms, land use, and vegetation that are not at all obvious at ground level.

Mountains are also excellent places to see a wide variety of plants. As altitude increases, temperature decreases; this means that there may be differences in vegetation from top to bottom. In general, plant communities adapted to cold climates are found at higher elevations, and those adapted to warmer climates are found at lower elevations. If you climb an Eastern mountain over 4000 feet in elevation, you'll find plants that you would normally have to travel hundreds of miles to the north to see.

Unlike the hard, dry masculinity of mountain tops, swamps have a soft, wet femininity that will put you in touch with the generative powers of nature. Bogs, another kind of wetland, are not as fertile as swamps, but they, too, leave little doubt as to what they are metaphorically about. Not many people know how to appreciate swamps and bogs, so in many areas you can enjoy them in privacy (Chapter 9).

SHORES

When you walk the shores of ponds and streams, you follow paths laid out by Nature herself. Ponds offer the advantage of circular walks—no backtracking required. In settled areas, however, your progress may be impeded by cabins and docks. Streams, due to their floodplains, are more apt to be free of houses and cabins, even in thickly settled areas. When walking around a large pond or lake, plan to be on an eastern shore in late afternoon so you can watch the sun go down *over* the water. And when walking a stream to see aquatic life, walk upstream. If you walk downstream, the current will carry news of your arrival (debris and disturbed sediment) ahead of you. (Similarly, when stalking terrestrial wildlife, walk upwind.)

Ponds are great places to sit at sunrise and sunset. Look for a seat that provides a wide view of the pond so that you can watch waterfowl coming and going. Old duck blinds and clear hillsides abutting the pond provide excellent seats.

During the heat of a summer day, sit *in* the pond. Find a sandy shore that's just deep enough to allow you to sit with only your head above water. Add a straw hat for dragon flies to perch on and let the minnows nibble at your toes. Hunker down now and then so that your ears are below the surface and listen to the cool sounds of the pond; then pop your head up and listen to the hot, airborne sounds of insects. That's what you call an *auricular hot-fudge sundae*.

You can also sit in a stream if it has deep pools, but shallow streams are best appreciated from a prone position. Find a sandy or gravelly stretch where the water is from 6 to 12 inches deep. Then lie down with your head upstream and your face to the sky. With your face above the water and everything else, including your ears, below, you'll be covered with a cool sheet and serenaded by the stream bed's glassy tinkle.

Conclusion

Taking a good walk is not as difficult as this chapter might suggest. Just remember that the whole law of walking is fulfilled in the first principle. Forget your obligations to society. Tight boots and black flies excepted, there is no problem so large that you can't walk away from it.

Thought Questions

1. Efficient walkers place their feet on the ground parallel to and almost coincident with their line of travel, rather than angling their feet in or out. Why?

Hint: Think of your feet as inchworms traveling along a stem. Each time one of them hits the ground, forces flow from heel, to arch, to ball, to toe, causing the foot to elongate. When your feet are parallel to the course you're traveling, forces will pass through them in line with their skeletal structure.

2. Many animals are *crepuscular,* so if you want to see them you'll have to become a crepuscular walker. How do you do that?

Hint: Animals that are active at night are said to be *nocturnal,* and those that are active during the day are said to be *diurnal.* But a great many animals are neither; they're most active during the two periods of twilight, dawn and dusk.

3. Some hunting coats are equipped with a waterproof flap that hangs from the back hem of the coat. This flap can be folded up, buttoned inside the coat, and used as a game pocket. But it's used for something else when it's left hanging. What?

Hint: Did you ever try to find a dry place to sit in the woods on a wet day in November? If your walking coat doesn't have a built-in seat, carry a square yard of waterproof nylon cloth.

4. Country children know that if you want to catch fireflies at night, it's best to crouch low to the ground and look up at the insects against the night sky. Why does this technique work, and what implications does it have for the night walker?

Hint: On most nights the sky is brighter than the ground or a backdrop of trees. Therefore, a firefly with its light off will show up better if you crouch down so as to silhouette its dark body against the relatively bright sky.

5. Thoreau claimed that a walker would be well served by learning to "shut every window with an apple tree." What did he mean?

   Hint: Concord, Massachusetts, was well settled even in Thoreau's day, and Thoreau knew that little good was likely to come from farmers and householders who spotted him enjoying their woods. So in order to avoid intrusions, he set a course that put an obstruction of some sort between himself and every window he passed.

Recommended Reading

BURROUGHS, JOHN. *Signs and Seasons.* Reprint edition, New York: Harper & Row, 1981. The first chapter, "A Sharp Lookout," is a practical essay on how to observe nature. Burroughs was a walker who knew how to sit.

KRESS, STEPHEN W. *The Audubon Society Handbook for Birders.* New York: Charles Scribner's Sons, 1981. See Chapter 3, "Observing Birds," if you want to learn how to keep field notes that meet rigorous scientific standards. Chapters 6, 7, and 8 contain listings that will help you locate local birding clubs, research organizations that welcome contributions from amateurs, and birding publications that pertain to your area.

LESLIE, CLARE WALKER. *Nature Drawing: A Tool for Learning.* Englewood Cliffs, New Jersey: Prentice-Hall, Inc., 1980. The author presents drawing as a direct way to study and appreciate nature. See especially Chapter 8, "Keeping a Field Sketchbook," in which she explains how to keep the classic field naturalist's notebook.

THOREAU, HENRY DAVID. *The Natural History Essays.* Edited with an introduction and notes by Robert Sattelmeyer. Salt Lake City, Utah: Peregrine Smith, Inc., 1980. This book contains "Walking" and seven other essays of interest to walkers. "Huckleberries," which is hard to find elsewhere, is among them.

EXCURSIONS

CHAPTER SIX
Night Wings

There are whole armies of living things, which, when we go to sleep, begin to awaken; and when we awaken, go to sleep. . . . Sunshine has much the same effect upon them as darkness has upon us. Our twilight is their morning; our midnight is their noonday.

W. J. Holland
The Moth Book 1903

Entomologists who study moths delight in taunting daytime naturalists with the observation, "Everything comes out at night." An
exaggeration? Perhaps, but moth experts spend a great deal of time
in the woods after dark, and they have developed gentle ways of
prodding nature into revealing creatures that normally remain hidden. Two of these techniques, *sugaring* and *running a sheet*, were
designed to collect moths, but they can be used to appreciate them
as well. Both techniques are explained below in terms of attracting
the large, beautiful moths known as the underwings, or *Catocala*.

The Catocala

Members of the genus *Catocala* are the big game of high-summer
mothing. Outspread, their *forewings* measure from 1½ to 3 inches,
and they're colored with subdued mixtures of whites, browns, and
grays in patterns that mimic tree bark. In sharp contrast, the *hind-
wings*, or *underwings*, are marked with bold colors and striking patterns (Figure 6-1). Hence, the genus name *Catocala*, from the
Greek words *kato*, meaning below, and *kalos*, meaning beautiful.
Catocala are found throughout the north temperate forests of the
world. In North America, where the genus arose, there are more
than 100 species, over seventy of which occur east of the Mississippi River.

Many woodland creatures find the *Catocala* just right for
hearty snacking. But before they can be eaten, they have to be
captured, and the *Catocala* have two lines of defense that help
prevent this from happening: a classic form of *cryptic coloration* and
a form of *flash coloration* of which any flimflam artist would be
proud.

Catocala spend the daylight hours snuggled close to tree trunks
and other plant surfaces, with their colorful underwings hidden
beneath their bark-colored forewings. Thus situated the moths are
extremely difficult to spot. This kind of camouflage is called cryptic
coloration, and the *Catocala* have developed it to a high degree.

If a predator should penetrate the cryptic defense of a
Catocala's forewings, the flash coloration of the underwings gives
the moth a second chance. When a resting *Catocala* is disturbed,

FIGURE 6-1. Three North American *Catocala*: (top) *C. parta*; (middle) *C. relicta*; (bottom) *C. amatrix*.

the boldly colored underwings appear in a flash from out of nowhere. This startling display, coupled with the mesmerizing on-and-off effect produced as the moth flutters away, alternately exposing and concealing its underwings, may confound a predatory jay or thrush long enough to allow the moth to escape.

DIET

The *Catocala* are so intimately connected to their food plants, they may be thought of as animated extensions of them. In addition to mimicking them both as adults and as caterpillars, some species of *Catocala* feed on only one species of plant. The sweet-fern underwing (*Catocala antinympha*), for example, feeds exclusively on the leaves of the sweet fern (*Myrica peregrina*). And as you might expect, the ranges of the shrub and the moth coincide. Although not all of the *Catocala* are quite so selective, the species present in an area are largely determined by the plants growing there. Basswood, oaks, hickories, walnuts, willows, poplars, cherries, and other deciduous trees and shrubs are some of their favorite food plants.

LIFE CYCLE

Winter finds the *Catocala* reduced to exquisitely sculptured eggs deposited on appropriate food plants. When the leaves of these plants appear in spring, the larvae hatch as caterpillars and immediately begin feeding on them. Like the adults, the caterpillars are nocturnal, feeding during the night and resting during the day. By early summer the full-grown caterpillars begin seeking sheltered locations on trees and on the forest floor in which to pupate. After a two- or three-week pupation period, the adults emerge as moths ready to begin the mating process. Unlike the voracious caterpillars, the adults are delicate feeders, subsisting primarily on nectars and saps.

During summer nights, while naturalists are distracting them with sugars and sheets, male and female *Catocala* are doing their best to find each other in the dark. The female "calls" males by perching on a trunk or branch, raising her abdomen, and releasing a chemical sex attractant, or *pheromone,* from its tip. The volatile pheromone streams through the night air with an occasional assist from the female's rapidly beating wings. Males, with their sensitive antennae at the ready, meander about seeking these perfumed streams, and when they locate one, they fly upstream to the source. Copulation occurs end to end. Shortly thereafter the female deposits as many as 100 eggs on the plants her larvae will feed on come spring.

Mothing Gear

You'll need the following items in order to set yourself up for a night of sugaring and sheeting:

> one electric headlamp
> one Coleman lantern
> three 20-foot pieces of $\frac{1}{4}$-inch rope
> two 5-foot pieces of $\frac{1}{4}$-inch rope
> two 24-inch stakes
> one white bedsheet
> two large safety pins
> one coffee can
> one small paintbrush
> two pounds of brown sugar
> twelve ounces of stale beer
> two rotten bananas

Dress for warm weather, but wear long pants and a long-sleeve shirt to thwart mosquitoes. Some people find that the required headlamp is more comfortable when worn over a cap. A cap will also prevent insects that buzz the headlamp from becoming entangled in your hair.

HEADLAMP

You may be able to purchase an electric headlamp locally at an outdoor store. If not, they're available from several of the mail-order outfitters listed in the Appendix.

If you're tempted to use a flashlight instead of a headlamp, resist the temptation; your mothing wouldn't suffer, but your experience of the night would. A headlamp opens the night without destroying it; a flashlight tears it apart. As you point it about, a flashlight will occasionally give you a blinding flash in the eye, and when your hands are busy and light is needed most, a flashlight is apt to be pointing off target. In comparison, wearing a headlamp is like having eyes that see in the dark. You don't see or handle the headlamp, yet its beam is welded to your line of sight. In fact, the light follows your gaze so smoothly, you soon forget that you're using a lamp.

A headlamp with either an adjustable or flood beam is ideal for mothing, because you'll be looking at things close at hand. Under these conditions the concentrated light of a spot beam is tiring. If you have a choice between a headlamp powered by a six-volt battery and a headlamp powered by C or D cells, bear in mind that six-volt batteries are more economical.

Many headlamps are poorly constructed, but with a soldering gun, insulated wire, and alligator clips you can improve them. First you may want to put longer wires on the lamp so you can carry the battery in your pack and still have enough slack wire to move your head freely. Alligator clips soldered to the battery ends of the new wires will prove to be more convenient than the washer-type terminal connectors that come with most six-volt headlamps. While you're at it, buy a spare bulb for your headlamp and keep it in your pack; that way you won't have to carry a flashlight as a backup.

Sugaring

Sugaring consists of attracting moths with a bait made of brown sugar, stale beer, and rotten fruit. In order to be successful at it, you must know where and when to sugar, how to prepare a far-calling bait, and how to run a bait line.

WHERE TO SUGAR

On your first mothing trip, aim at attracting a variety of *Catocala* so as to maximize your chances of seeing at least some. Choose a mixed hardwood forest containing many different food plants. After you've had some experience sugaring, you can become selective and aim for a particular species of *Catocala*. In that case, use one of the books listed at the end of this chapter to find out what your chosen moth's favorite larval food plant is; then locate an area where the plant is abundant and go mothing there.

The forest you choose for your first mothing trip should have a clear path running through it. Sugared bait is set by dabbing small patches of it on tree trunks. If the trees are along a clear path, it's easy to keep track of them in the dark. Until you learn to recognize good mothing habitat, a path that runs through several different habitats is to be preferred over a path that runs through only one or two. Also, bear in mind that the *Catocala* have been dealing with bats, whippoorwills, and other flying predators for aeons, so they generally avoid open spaces far from cover.

WHEN TO SUGAR

Nights too hot and muggy for sleeping are excellent for mothing. Clouds and even a light mist are fine; they limit the amount of heat that is lost to radiant cooling. Should the temperature drop below the *dew point* during the night—it has if you can see your breath—moth activity will decrease sharply. A light breeze is tolerable, but moths don't like to fly in strong winds.

The *Catocala* season runs from late July until early September, prime time being the dog days of late summer. But the *Catocala* season is only one of several sugaring seasons, and you may want to try some of the others. In terms of numbers alone, the most productive time for sugaring is from April to early May. The fragrance of your bait will have little competition from flowering plants at that time, and moths of many kinds may come in droves. (But the *Catocala* won't be among them, because in April and May they exist as eggs or caterpillars.) Activity at your bait will taper off as competition from flowering plants increases, reaching a low point in June and July, and then picking up again with the late-summer *Catocala* season. The first frost signals the end of the *Catocala* season and the beginning of the last peak period of the mothing year. Moths that winter as adults become extremely active on mild nights after the first frost as they fly about seeking a last meal before bedding down for the winter.

BAIT

When mothing you're only as good as your bait. The literature is full of recipes, some of which call for exotic sugar, old rum, and expensive French perfume. Collectors, however, generally agree on the following basic ingredients: brown sugar, stale beer, and rotten fruit. The idea is to create a mixture that is both aromatic and sweet. The aroma attracts the moths, and the sugar—which they eat—keeps them around. The mixture should be viscous enough to stay put when painted on a tree.

In *Legion of Night: The Underwing Moths* (see Recommended Reading), Theodore D. Sargent claims that two pounds of brown sugar dissolved in six ounces of stale beer works as well as any bait. Others prefer to dissolve the brown sugar in an aged mixture of stale beer, rotting bananas or peaches, and a dollop or two of cola. Whatever you decide to use, dissolve the sugar over low heat so as not to drive off all of the aromatic substances in your bait.

If you don't want to leave anything to chance—anything, that is, except your health, your home, and your car—once you get into the field add a few drops of *phenyl acetaldehyde* to the evening's bait supply. Phenyl acetaldehyde is used in some perfumes, and just a few drops will fill the woods with a flowery odor. Because of its strength, it must be used with extreme caution. A spill of several drops could render a room or an automobile off limits for an indefinite period. In its concentrated form, phenyl acetaldehyde is a hazard to health; don't inhale it or get it on your skin, and don't use it when mothing with children.

Running a Bait Line. By six or seven o'clock in the evening you should be able to predict the night's weather. If it looks good for sugaring, leave your house in time to arrive at your mothing spot before dark.

When you arrive, walk along the path you plan to sugar and select your bait trees. Trees should be no more than from 15 to 40 feet apart; otherwise it's difficult to keep track of them, because large gaps between bait trees can be disorienting. Thin strips torn from an old bedsheet and tied to each bait tree or simply placed on the trail in front of each bait tree will help you relocate the trees later on. Plan on baiting from twenty to thirty trees your first night out.

A coffee can makes a good bait container, especially if you punch two holes near the top and affix a wire bail to it. Since sugared bait is messy stuff, it's best to carry the can less than half full. A 1-inch paintbrush makes a good applicator.

Start baiting your trees at dusk by painting a 3- by 5-inch patch on each tree at breast height (Figure 6-2). This height will enable you to observe moths in comfort. You may find that some species make better bait trees than others. Some sugarers, for example, avoid conifers. Whichever trees you use, be generous with your bait.

Wait until dark to run your first check. After that you can develop a pleasant rhythm by checking your trees at regular intervals. If it takes you thirty minutes to check your bait line and you rest for fifteen minutes between checks, you'll begin a new check every forty-five minutes. Of course, your rounds will take much longer on good nights when there are many moths to look at.

Catocala are sensitive to light, so when you approach a bait tree, don't look directly at the bait. If you do, your headlamp's beam will disturb the moths before you get close enough to observe them. Keep your eyes—and light—on the trail until you're standing before the tree; then examine the trunk from the bottom up. Moths hit by a light will sometimes flutter to the ground, so if you look from the top down, the first moth to drop will disturb all of the others.

Mothing is a thing of uncertainties. Even with excellent bait, a good location, and a hot night, you may not see any *Catocala*. This uncertainty is one of the attractions of mothing. Molecules of your aromatic bait will be carried to nooks and crannies throughout the woods. How many dim, mothy brains will the aroma encounter, and how many of these will be drawn to your bait? Why do moths appear on some nights and not on others? What else besides

FIGURE 6-2. Baiting a tree.

moths and a flying squirrel or two will come out of the darkness? These are the kinds of questions to savor as you sit enjoying the mixture of satisfaction and anticipation that trappers the world over and through all time have known. You've done what you can; now it's nature's move.

CATOCALA AT BAIT

Catocala at bait provide one of the most enchanting visual displays the north temperate forests have to offer. Imagine a cloud of twenty or thirty 3-inch _Catocala_ circling the bait, some landing, others taking flight, iridescent eyes blazing red, and underwings flashing in typical _Catocala_ fashion, giving the whole a pulse as if it were one being. The total effect is compounded by the eerie silence of moths in flight and the persistent retinal afterimages produced by viewing brightly illuminated colors against a black background.

After seeing the _Catocala_ of your region for the first time, you may feel somewhat ashamed at having ignored these softly magnificent creatures for so long. Rather than chastise yourself, make up for lost time. Find a comfortable spot close to a busy bait tree and have a seat. Dip the fingers of both hands into the bait (assuming there's no phenyl acetaldehyde in it) and anoint your forehead. Then cross your forearms and bring your baited hands to rest on your shoulders. Relax and invite the _Catocala_ to brush their soft wings against your face and to perch where they will, while concepts such as "insect" and "bug" drift off into the night.

Instead of becoming a bait tree, you may prefer to sit at the base of one that already has _Catocala_ on it. After a while the moths will flutter back to the bait, and your head will be wreathed with _Catocala_.

The tree you choose to sit in front of may come in handy as a backrest. The genus _Catocala_ is in the family Noctuidae, and one of the members of this family is a dark-colored moth, with a 6-inch wingspread, called the Black Witch (_Ascalpha odorata_). These dark beauties are infrequent visitors to northern forests, but if one should fly out of the night and land on your face, the tree will keep you from hitting your head on a rock as you fall back in a swoon.

Running a Sheet

Sugaring is an effective technique for attracting *Catocala* and other moths that enjoy an occasional sip of nectar, but not all moths do, and those that don't rarely show up at bait trees. Unfortunately, the abstainers include some large, showy moths, such as the luna moth (*Actias luna*), the prometheus moth (*Callosamia promethea*), and other members of the family Saturniidae. But these beauties will come to light and you can "attract" them (see Thought Question 1) with an illuminated bedsheet. A sheet will also attract many other varieties of moths, including the *Catocala*.

To set up a sheet, select two trees that stand 4 to 10 feet apart. Tie one rope between the two trees 6 feet above the ground, and tie another rope between the two trees $1\frac{1}{2}$ feet above the ground. Be sure the ropes are taut.

After the ropes are in place, fold a twin-bed sheet in half lengthwise. When folded it will measure approximately 3 feet by 9 feet. Hold the folded sheet lengthwise and drape the top foot or two over the upper rope. Then use two safety pins to secure the sheet in place. The side of the sheet with the flap on it will become the back of your mothing sheet, and the unobstructed side will become the front.

Next, drive two stakes into the ground approximately 4 feet in front of the lower tree rope and approximately 4 feet apart. Tie a 5-foot piece of rope to each of the two bottom corners of the sheet, and with the sheet draped behind the lower tree rope, pull the ropes attached to the sheet under the lower tree rope. Then tie each of the sheet ropes to the stake in front of it. This will produce a raised, horizontal shelf in front of the sheet (Figure 6-3).

Many entomologists and collectors use sheets, but the shelf configuration described above was developed by Professor John C. Franclemont at Cornell University. His students call it the *Franclemont sheet*, and although it takes a bit longer than a straight sheet to set up, it has definite advantages. If the bottom of a sheet is allowed to rest on the ground, moths that become confused and fall may be lost in the folds of the sheet or on the forest floor. The shelf provides a resting place for confused moths and a convenient viewing surface for collectors. In addition, the open space beneath the

FIGURE 6-3. An illuminated mothing sheet in place.

shelf allows moths that flutter down the rear of the sheet to regain flight before they hit the ground. This keeps them circulating about the sheet.

With luck and planning there may be a convenient branch from which to suspend a Coleman lantern approximately 2 feet below the top of the sheet and 1 or 2 feet from its front surface. The lantern will illuminate both sides of the sheet, and in a short time there will be moths and other night-flying insects all over it.

Ultraviolet lamps are *far* more effective than Coleman lanterns, and many collectors use them. So if mothing becomes one of your regular activities, you may want to rig up a battery-powered ultraviolet lamp, or you can buy one ready-made. Two mail-order sources are listed in the Appendix.

Sheets have long-range drawing power, so place yours in a spot where it will be exposed to several habitats. For example, if you set up at the edge of a woods bordering an overgrown field, you'll draw moths from both the woods and the field. The large Saturniidae fly in June, so you'll definitely want to do some sheeting then, but you can also take your sheet along on August nights when you're sugaring for *Catocala*. In addition to attracting insects that don't come to bait, an illuminated sheet adds a cheery glow to a mothing camp.

Conclusion

Sugaring and running a sheet are excellent ways to attract and capture moths and other night-flying insects, but they offer the qualitative naturalist even more. They open the night to exploration, and in much the same way that a bird feeder serves the birder, they make it possible to appreciate moths without destroying them.

Thought Questions

1. Popular belief has it that moths are *attracted* to light, but recent scientific work suggests that the opposite may be true. Professor Henry S. Hsiao (see Recommended Reading) believes that the nature of a moth's eyes and nervous system may cause it to fly toward light which it is actually trying to avoid. This novel theory is called the "Mach band hypothesis," and it is based on work done by Ernst Mach in the 1860s. Mach discovered that the human eye physiologically enhances the boundaries between light and dark areas in the field of vision by making the boundaries of the light areas lighter and the boundaries of the dark areas darker. These physiologically produced light and dark bands (Mach bands) increase visual acuity in much the same way as does outlining a pictured object with a black pen.

Although it has not been determined whether moths perceive Mach bands, Professor Hsiao assumes that they do, and he explains their *apparent* attraction to light as follows. A moth in the vicinity of a light bulb in the woods at night sees a light area (the bulb) and a dark area (the woods). Assuming that the moth is *negatively phototropic*, as many nocturnal creatures are, it will seek to avoid the light by flying toward the darkest area in sight. Ironically, the darkest area in the moth's field of vision is the physiologically produced Mach band bordering the bulb, so it flies toward it. To the human observer, the hapless moth appears to be attracted to the light, when in fact it is seeking darkness. (For reasons that need not concern us here, the moth's eyes and nervous system serve it well when confronted with natural sources of light such as the sun and the moon; problems arise only in the vicinity of relatively weak sources of artificial light.)

No doubt you've watched moths in the vicinity of light bulbs many times. What have you observed about their behavior that would provide circumstantial evidence in favor of Professor Hsiao's Mach band hypothesis?

Hint: What is the flight path of a moth in the vicinity of a light bulb? If moths are truly attracted to light, one would expect them to approach a bulb in a straight line or something close to it. If, on the other hand, the Mach band hypothesis is correct, one would expect moths to fly around a bulb as they repeatedly aim for the Mach band that appears to be a very dark area bordering it.

Where do moths come to rest near a light bulb? If they are truly attracted to light, one would expect them to land close to the bulb and bask in its light. If the Mach band hypothesis is correct, one would expect moths to settle in dark nooks and crannies near the bulb. Tack a crumpled piece of black paper on the side of your house near the porch light and see what happens.

2. Bright tail ends and subdued front ends are not unique to the *Catocala*; consider, for example, the cottontail rabbit and the white-tailed deer. In addition to startling predators, how else might a brightly colored tail end help a moth or other animal avoid capture?

Hint: Ask a cottontail rabbit hunter whether he or she misses more cottontails by shooting ahead of them or behind them as they dash straightaway. Similarly, what do you suppose an *unsuccessful* mountain lion aims at when lunging after a white-tailed deer?

3. A considerate person will not look you in the eye during a mothing trip. Why not?

Hint: Put on your headlamp and adjust it for mothing, light on and angled downward for viewing nearby objects. Then, go into a dark bathroom, stand in front of the mirror, and look yourself in the eye.

4. Cats, raccoons, and some other nocturnal prowlers are easy to spot at night because their eyes glow green or red when hit with a light. Your own eyes, and those of many other diurnal creatures, don't "glow in the dark." Explain.

Hint: A cat's eye contains a reflective layer of cells called a *tapetum lucidum*, which directs light onto the retina, thereby increasing the cat's ability to see in low-light situations.

5. Moths, warblers, Canada geese, and many other creatures often do their serious flying at night. Why?

Hint: These creatures fly at night for the same reason wilderness canoeists will sometimes wait until evening to cross a large stretch of open water.

Recommended Reading

ALLEN, P. B. M. *A Moth Hunter's Gossip.* London: Philip Alan and Co. Ltd., 1937. This book was intended to entertain, but it instructs as well. See Chapter 4 ("Sugar and East Winds") for tips on how to use light winds to your advantage. Allen demonstrates how far moth appreciation can go, and his writings suggest why the English have been called a "nation of naturalists."

DIRIG, ROBERT. *Growing Moths* (4-H Member's Guide M-6-6). Ithaca: New York State College of Agriculture and Life Sciences, 1975. Available at minimal cost from Distribution Center, 7 Research Park, Cornell University, Ithaca, New York, 14850. This thirty-nine-page booklet provides a good introduction to moths and mothing, and it includes detailed instructions for rearing over twenty-five species.

HOLLAND, W. J. *The Moth Book.* New York: Doubleday, 1903; reprint edition, New York: Dover Publications, Inc., 1968. This has been the handbook for North American moth collectors since its publication. Approximately 1500 species of moths are pictured in full color; information on ranges, food plants, and life cycles is given; and the text is peppered with quotations on moths gleaned from a wide variety of sources.

HSIAO, HENRY S. *Attraction of Moths to Light and to Infrared Radiation.* San Francisco: San Francisco Press, Inc., 1972. This is the book in which Professor Hsiao puts forth the Mach band hypothesis. It's a scientific report and much of it is beyond the scope of the lay reader. However, parts of section 3 ("The Attraction of Moths to Visible Light") read like a detective story, and they provide good examples of the way scientists work.

MITCHELL, ROBERT T. and ZIM, S. HERBERT. *Butterflies and Moths.* New York: Golden Press, 1977. A handy picture guide to common moths and butterflies with information on ranges, food plants, and life histories.

SARGENT, THEODORE D. *Legion of Night: The Underwing Moths.* Amherst: The University of Massachusetts Press, 1976. The author intended this book to be a "popular, up-to-date, and comprehensive treatment of the *Catocala* of eastern North America," and it is. Seventy-one species are described and pictured in full color, and the natural history of each is given. *The* book for *Catocala* enthusiasts and a fine book for any naturalist.

CHAPTER SEVEN

North American Gold

To the entomologist the goldenrod is a rich mine, yielding
to the collector more treasures than any other flower. It
gives up its gold-dust pollen to every insect-seeker; and
because of this generous attitude to all-comers it is truly
emblematic of the country that has chosen it
as its national flower.

John Henry Comstock and
Anna Botsford Comstock
Manual for the Study of Insects, 1897

The goldenrods are so widespread and so much a part of the North American landscape, that in the late nineteenth century there was a movement to make them the national flower of the United States. The movement failed, despite what the Comstocks say above, in part because some feared that adoption of the goldenrod would suggest a nation preoccupied with gold of the mineral kind. Nonetheless, the goldenrods are natives of North America, and unlike Queen Anne's lace, purple loosestrife, and some of the other beautiful aliens that color our roadsides in August, they are distinctly North American in character.

Natives or not, the goldenrods are generally under-appreciated for a number of extraneous reasons. Goldenrods are ubiquitous, and they bloom in late summer when there are many other flowers, fruits, and brightly colored leaves to distract the naturalist. These factors make it all too easy to cut through a field of goldenrods seeing nothing but the wild apples on the other side.

In addition, before we get to know the goldenrods some of us are turned against them by hearsay branding them as the cause of hay fever. That's misleading because autumnal allergies are actually caused by wind-borne pollens from plants such as ragweed. Goldenrod pollen is too heavy to ride the wind; insects carry it from plant to plant. In fact, when atmospheric pollen was analyzed in New York at the peak of the fall allergy season, goldenrod pollen was found to account for only 1 to 2 percent of the total.

Finally, though rich and complex, the goldenrod community is composed of small and often subtle elements, so it takes know-how to appreciate it. But those who have the know-how will find enough in a field of goldenrods to keep them occupied for a lifetime of autumns. This chapter will get you started by introducing the single most common species of goldenrod and some of the insects associated with it, particularly that bizarre yet homey group, the gall-makers.

The Canada Goldenrod

When you look at a field of goldenrods in eastern North America, you may be seeing as many as five or six different species. There are approximately 125 species of goldenrods in all, seventy of which can be found east of the Mississippi River. The species present in any given field are determined by location, soil type, drainage, pH (acidity or alkalinity of the soil), time since abandonment, and various other factors. But if the field you're looking at is relatively fertile and neither too dry nor too wet, you can be fairly certain that some of the plants are Canada goldenrods (*Solidago canadensis*). (Not all goldenrods grow in fields. There are also such woodland species as the zigzag goldenrod and the silver-rod, the only member of the genus with white flowers.)

The Canada goldenrod stands straight and tall, sometimes as high as 5 feet (Figure 7-1). The stem is round with occasional ridges, the upper half is covered with fine hairs, and the lower half is bare. Leaves are 3 to 6 inches long and $\frac{3}{8}$ to $\frac{7}{8}$ of an inch wide, tapered at both ends, and noticeably toothed. Each leaf has *three* main veins, a relatively smooth top, and a bottom made rough by hairs that are especially dense along the veins. The leaves are the same shape throughout the plant, but they are smaller at the top, and as the plant matures, the large lower leaves shrivel up and fall off. Flowers occur in a pyramidal head at the top of the plant. Each head is from 4 to 16 inches long and is composed of tiny flowers attached to recurved branches that radiate off a central stem.

The best way to differentiate the Canada goldenrod from other goldenrod species is with the aid of a field guide. A good field guide will point out morphological differences between species. For example, the lance-leaved, or grass-leaved, goldenrod (*Solidago graminifolia*) often grows alongside the Canada goldenrod, but you can tell the two apart by the former's narrow, smooth-edged leaves and flat-topped flower clusters. Similarly, the rough-stemmed goldenrod (*Solidago rugosa*), which looks very much like the Canada goldenrod, can be distinguished by its *very* hairy stem, rough leaves, and the *single* main vein in each leaf.

The reproductive habits of the Canada goldenrod provide another clue to its identity. Although they reproduce sexually with small, wind-blown seeds called *achenes*, they also reproduce asexually with underground stems called *rhizomes*. Once a solitary plant is established, rhizomes spread out from it in all directions. Shoots develop on the rhizomes in autumn, and come spring they produce

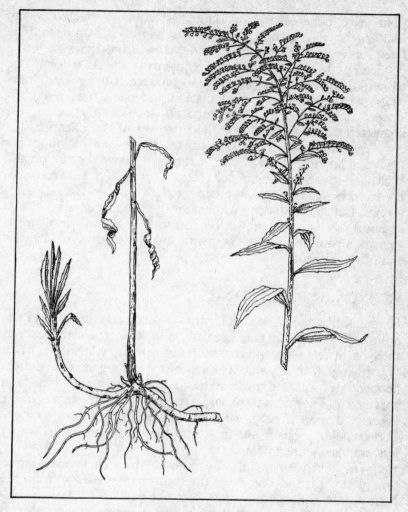

FIGURE 7-1. Canada goldenrod (*Solidago canadensis*) in flower.

upright stems. After several seasons a clump of many stems develops. These clumps are called *clones* because all of the plants in a clump have the same genetic makeup.

You may be able to spot clones of Canada goldenrod in mixed fields by looking for distinct, round clumps of tall plants with stems from 3 to 6 inches apart. Since clonal growth is an effective way to limit interspecific competition, these clumps will often be entirely free of other plants. In virgin prairie, clones sometimes grew to a diameter of 30 feet, and as the older plants in the center of a large clone died, grasses replaced them to produce huge, golden "fairy rings" which must have both pleased and puzzled westering pioneers. Other species of goldenrod also produce clones, so this characteristic alone is not a sufficient means of identification.

If you want to be fairly sure that the plant you're looking at is a Canada goldenrod, look for one that fits the above description and that has a round swelling or *ball gall* on its stem. The flies responsible for these galls most often deposit their eggs on Canada goldenrods. But they also deposit them on the late goldenrod (*Solidago gigantea*), so ball galls appear on this species as well. In general, though, a ball gall on a plant growing in a well-drained field means Canada goldenrod.

ECONOMIC IMPORTANCE

Economically, the Canada goldenrod occupies an enviable and safe positon: It's generally perceived to be useless. In North America there is little or no interest in harvesting it, cultivating it, or "improving" it in any way. Natural history writers don't even recommend its leaves for tea, and they'll decoct almost anything for a paragraph. (They do recommend a tea made from the leaves of the sweet goldenrod [*Solidago odorata*].) Thus, in its native land the Canada goldenrod is free to grow unmolested in hedgerows, vacant lots, and abandoned fields.

The North American goldenrods have received greater attention abroad than at home. As the genus name *Solidago* (from the Latin *solidus* and *ago*, meaning "to make whole") indicates, goldenrods were once thought to have curative powers. In the early part of the seventeenth century, Canada goldenrods were dried and shipped to Great Britain and Europe, where they were sold by the ounce. Medicinal interest in them waned when goldenrods were discovered growing in the woods of England. The seventeenth-century English herbalist John Gerade, as quoted by Charlotte

Erichsen-Brown in *Use of Plants* (Aurora, Ontario: Breezy Creek Press, 1979), tells the story:

> It, the Goldenrod, is extolled above all other herbes for the stopping of bloud in sanguinolent ulcers and bleeding wounds; and hath in times past beene had in greater estimation and regard than in these dayes: for in my remembrance I have known the dry herbe which came from beyond the sea sold . . . for halfe a crown an ounce. But once it was found in Hampstead wood . . . no man will give halfe a crown for a hundred weight of it . . . esteeming no longer of anything, how pretious so ever it may be, than whilst it is strange and rare.

In any age, the value of the commonplace is hard to see.

Today, North American goldenrods still receive some attention abroad. *Cultivars* (varieties of plants that have been produced through cultivation) of Canada goldenrod, with names such as Golden Wings and Goldenmosa, are grown as ornamentals by gardeners in Great Britain. And in Japan, where Canada goldenrod grows as an alien weed, beekeepers who appreciate it as a source of nectar have distributed it widely.

Assassins and Bushwackers

Although the Canada goldenrod does not play a major role in the human community, it plays a vitally important role as a primary producer in old-field biological communities. As a primary producer, the Canada goldenrod photosynthetically converts simple substances into plant parts that serve as food for a wide variety of creatures, particularly insects. In fact, when goldenrod fields are going at full tilt in the late-summer sun, they chirp, hum, and buzz with insect sounds. One naturalist collected 241 species of insects on Canada goldenrods in a single season. Examine a clone and you'll discover a number of gentle grazers and fierce predators.

Leave your net at home and go eyeball to eyeball with the insects. A healthy clone of Canada goldenrods is conveniently close to chin high, so you can observe insects with ease. If you like, take along a baby-food jar, and when you see an insect you wish to examine closely, capture it with the jar. Come at the insect from below with the open jar. Then, when the insect is in the jar, or just about to be, clap the lid on. If all you want is a survey of the insects present, *sweeping* through the clone with an insect net is the technique to use. But sweeping injures many insects, and in terms of behavioral studies it reveals more about how insects respond to nets than about how insects respond to goldenrods and each other. Direct observation is still a good way to learn about insects and goldenrods, and on those rare occasions when you want to capture an insect, you'll find a baby-food jar far more sporting than a net. The following are seven insects you're almost sure to see.

WHITE-FACED HORNET

For all their mean magnificence, in terms of looks alone, jet fighters have nothing on the white-faced hornet (*Vespula maculata*). When you spot one of these black and white beauties on a flower head, overcome your initial desire to back off and ease as close to it as you dare (Figure 7-2). The hornet is feeding on nectar, and when it has had enough, it will tilt off the flower, drop just a bit—like a fighter leaving a carrier deck—and level off in the direction of the next goldenrod. In "Waspish," Robert Frost (*The Poetry of Robert Frost*. New York: Holt, Rhinehart and Winston, 1969) was talking about another wasp, not the white-faced hornet, when he wrote:

> Poor egotist, he has no way of knowing,
> But he's as good as anybody going.

Unlike Frost's "poor egotist," the white-faced hornet knows! (For Frost's observations on the white-faced hornet, see his poem "The White-Tailed Hornet.")

PAPER WASPS

The paper wasps (*Polistes sp.*) are closely related to the white-faced hornets, but they are far less bellicose. In fact, these common brown hornets are good natured, particularly when full of goldenrod

FIGURE 7-2. Six insects commonly found on Canada goldenrod: (a) honeybee; (b) white-faced hornet; (c) paper wasp; (d) ambush bug; (e) striped goldenrod beetle; (f) assassin bug.

nectar. Like other wasps and hornets, only the females sting, but unlike the others, it's easy to tell the males from the females. The females have brown faces and the tips of their antennae are straight. The males have yellow faces and candy-cane shaped antennae, which differ markedly from the brown faces and relatively straight antennae of the females (Figure 7-2). Look several of these wasps in the face and you'll see the difference.

This writer would never suggest that you do so foolish a thing as to put the above piece of knowledge to the test. After all, with such a brief description it would be impossible to identify a paper wasp with any degree of certainty, and although picking up wasps with your bare hands might impress your companions, it's the kind of grandstanding that conscientious naturalists avoid. Nevertheless, someday when you're alone in a field of goldenrods and there is no pressure on you, find a male paper wasp. Then ask yourself the following two questions: (1) How much of what I read do I really believe? and (2) Which is stronger, my gut-level fear of wasps or my intellectual understanding of them?

HONEYBEES

Although itself an alien, the honeybee (family Apidae)—or as the American Indians called it, "the white man's fly"—has become a fast friend of the native Canada goldenrod (Figure 7-2). The two look so compatible together, one wonders what the goldenrods did for excitement before the honeybees arrived. (The bumblebees were here to entertain them.) Note that honeybees enjoy pollen as well as nectar.

A local beekeeper may be able to supply you with a bottle of goldenrod honey. You'll find it thick, smooth, and flavorful, with a golden color reminiscent of the blossoms themselves. Some connoisseurs consider it the ideal honey, especially after it has been aged and thoroughly ripened.

AMBUSH BUG

One of the most appalling sights you're apt to see amid the goldenrods is the body of a honeybee draped over the side of a flower head, pollen sacks hanging sadly by its sides. Look closer and you'll see a mottled, yellow bug holding the bee's thorax. This bush-wacker is called an ambush bug (family Phymatidae). It lies hidden among the goldenrod's blossoms waiting for other insects to come within striking distance. When they do, the ambush bug over-powers them with its tanklike body and massive front legs (Figure 7-2).

ASSASSIN BUG

Another predator you're likely to see on goldenrod blossoms is the assassin bug (family Reduviidae). Compared with the ambush bug, the assassin bug is sleek and elegant (Figure 7-2). Even its beak, which it, too, uses to suck liquids from insect prey, is thin and hairlike. Normally it's kept tucked in a groove under the body, but you can get a glimpse of it by looking down on an assassin bug. When the bug lifts its head to look back at you, the beak will be partly exposed. Their habit of looking up and around gives the assassins an intelligent, companionable air. Handle them with care nonetheless; some can inflict painful stings with their beaks. (One southern member of this family hides in bedclothes and sucks human blood.)

STRIPED GOLDENROD BEETLE

Goldenrod leaves riddled with holes are a sign of the striped gold-enrod beetle (_Trirhabda sp._) (Figure 7-2). These beetles are com-mitted to the goldenrod from birth onward. Only one generation per year is produced, and the larvae appear just in time to feed on the tender shoots of new goldenrods. Even as adults they prefer tender leaves, so in autumn you'll find them high on the plants where the leaves are still relatively young and tender. When danger threatens, striped goldenrod beetles employ an age-old defense: they drop out of sight for a while. Worry a group of them by jiggling the plant they're feeding on and watch what happens. After the bail-out, try to find one in the grass below the plant.

OTHER INSECTS AND SPIDERS

In addition to the insects mentioned above, you'll see other arthropods. These include aphids, praying mantises, blister beetles, locust borers, northern corn rootworm beetles, soldier beetles, tarnished plant bugs, crab spiders, orb-weaving spiders, monarch butterflies fueling up for the trip south, and scores more. You'll also see the snug homes of the gall-makers.

The Gall-Makers

HOUSES AND DOORS

As intelligent creatures who dwell in houses, we are naturally sympathetic to others who do the same. I mean *houses*, not nests or webs, but real houses with stout walls, roofs, and doors. Doors most of all, because on this planet privacy is at a premium, and doors make privacy possible. Doors allow living creatures to be themselves, vulnerable yet safe, in private worlds within the world.

Houses are few in the woods. The inhabited holes you sometimes see in forest trees come close to being houses; all they lack are doors. Woodchuck burrows also come close, but entrances, even two, three, or four of them, don't equal one door. A muskrat's lodge might qualify as a house if one were willing to call the water covering the entrance a door, but the mink who eat muskrats don't stop to knock, so the best we can say is that the muskrat lives in an elevated burrow. You and I, the goldenrod gall fly (*Eurosta solidaginis*), the goldenrod elliptical gall moth (*Gnorimoschema gallaesolidaginus*), and the scarred goldenrod gall moth (*Encosma scudderiana*) live in houses; significant parts of our lives are spent behind closed doors.

GOLDENROD BALL GALLS

Ball galls are the round swellings you see on the stems of some Canada goldenrods (Figure 7-3). One is the usual number per stem, but stems with two are common. Stems with three are harder to find. Stems with four have been found, and there are naturalists

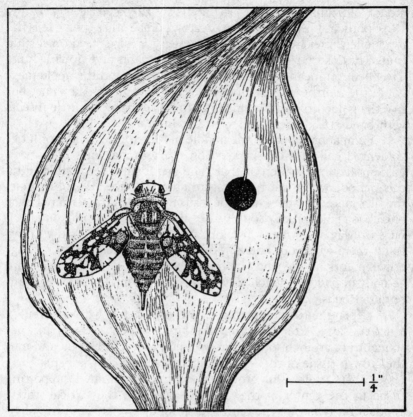

FIGURE 7-3. Ball gall and ball gall fly.

who believe that somewhere there is a stem with five perfectly formed ball galls on it. The limited growing season in the Canada goldenrod's range and the life cycle of the gall fly suggest that a stem with five perfect ball galls is unlikely, but black pearls and ambergris notwithstanding, what a prize such a stem would be.

THE GOLDENROD GALL FLY

The goldenrod gall fly, the insect responsible for ball galls, is one of the true _fruit flies_ (family Tephritidae). The "fruit fly" that flits around old bananas and biology labs is actually a *pomace fly* (family Drosophilidae). As the name indicates, pomace flies (pomace is the residue left after fruits have been pressed for juice) feed on rotting fruit, whereas true fruit flies feed on living plants and growing fruit. The Mediterranean fruit fly of California fame and the apple maggot of the Northeast have given the true fruit flies a bad name, but like the goldenrod gall fly, many of them are beautiful little insects with banded abdomens and spotted wings.

From approximately the middle of May to the middle of June, goldenrod gall flies can be seen on the terminal buds of Canada goldenrod stems, which at that time are about 2 feet tall. During this period, when the temperature climbs above 70° Fahrenheit, the flies mate, and the female deposits her eggs in the terminal buds of Canada goldenrods. You may see the flies in action if you check buds in May and June. On cool days they're sluggish and you can catch them with your hands. The females are the ones with sting-erlike points at the ends of their abdomens. The "stingers" are actually *ovipositors*, which the females use to inject their eggs into terminal buds.

Depending on temperature, the eggs hatch within seven to fourteen days. After hatching, the larva, which is less than one-sixteenth of an inch long, burrows down through the bud and into the growth tissue of the stem. There it eats out a chamber slightly larger than itself. Only the *pith*, or undifferentiated supporting tissue in the center of the stem, is damaged; the critical water-conduction tissues of the outer stem are left intact. And the plant continues to grow normally, except for a *cecidia*, or gall, which forms around the larva's chamber, evidently in response to secretions given off by the larva. Developing galls are first visible in late June.

The larva spends the summer in the gall feeding primarily on plant juices, some of which are absorbed directly through the body wall. Other than the gall itself, the larva's activity does little apparent damage to the plant, but plants with galls typically produce fewer flowers, achenes, and new rhizomes.

Open a gall in August and you'll find a fat, white larva, technically called a *maggot*, inside. To open a gall, cut around its equator to a depth of a quarter of an inch; then snap the two hemispheres apart by twisting your knife blade in the cut. The two black prongs at the anterior end of the larva are its *mouth hooks.* The tan marks at the posterior end are part of the respiratory system. Note the gray-green waste material packed in the lower part of the chamber. Unfortunately, once you have dispossessed a larva in this way, about all you can do is place the larva and its broken house on the ground and hope that the Fates will be kinder to you.

Cut another gall open in mid-September and you'll see that the larva has begun to excavate a tunnel from its chamber to the outside. Most often these tunnels are made somewhere in the upper half, or *dome,* of the gall. (The lower half of the gall is called the *hold.*) By late October the tunnel will have been completed all the way to, but not through, the gall's outer layer of cells, or *epidermis.* In effect, the larva has constructed a hallway and a door to the outside world. (These closed doors are almost impossible to spot from the outside, but you can locate them by systematically pricking the surface of the gall with a pin.) Hallway and door completed, the larva retires to the central chamber and prepares for winter.

When the goldenrod withers in late fall, the walls of the gall turn tough and corky. During the winter these thick walls protect the dormant larva from rapid changes in temperature. But they can't protect the larva from freezing temperatures, so before going into dormancy the larva decreases the amount of water in its body. This causes it to shrink in size, and it prevents the formation of destructive ice crystals in the larva's cells.

Come spring, the larva awakens and begins to pupate, and by April or May an adult fly is ready to emerge. Now the wisdom of the industrious larva becomes apparent. Unlike the larva, the adult fly does not have the mouth hooks needed to dig its way out of the tough, dry gall. If a hallway and door were not already in place, the adult would die trapped in the central chamber.

As it is, all the adult fly has to do is break through the weathered and weakened layer of cells forming the door. This it does with an inflatable battering ram called a *ptilinum,* a fleshy, bladderlike structure on the fly's head. The fly pushes the ptilinum against the door until the door bursts open leaving the small (one-eighth of an inch in diameter) round hole you see in many old galls. Once out of the gall, the ptilinum is retracted, never to be used again. Meanwhile, the body of the fly hardens, and its wings expand to their full size. All this occurs within thirty minutes while the fly is perched on the gall from which it emerged. If you gather a bouquet of galls just before the process begins, you can watch it happen. The adult fly lives for several weeks, during which time mating occurs and the cycle begins again.

PARASITES

Marauding naturalists are not the only creatures the larva has to fear. If you open ten ball galls in late October, you'll almost certainly find one or two with a brown pupal case inside. Note, too, that the usual white larva, hallway, and door are lacking—sure signs that the larva has been parasitized and consumed by a parasitic wasp (*Eurytoma obtusiventris*) about the size of the fly. Evidently, the female wasp implants her egg in the fly larva during May and June before the larva leaves the terminal bud. This causes the larva to pupate prematurely, and when it does, the newly hatched wasp larva consumes the fly larva from within! Thus, the premature pupal case you find in autumn is that of a goldenrod gall fly, but it contains the larva of a parasitic wasp. The wasp larva winters in the pupal case and emerges in the spring. Unlike the adult goldenrod gall fly, the adult wasp has chewing mouth parts, so it is able to gnaw its way out of the gall.

Some of the galls that you open in late October may contain a larger-than-normal central chamber, a strange larva, and a mass of dark, granular material. Again, the hallway and exit door will be lacking. Examine the larva and you'll find that its posterior end is sharply tapered. These signs indicate that the goldenrod gall fly larva was parasitized and consumed by another small wasp: *Eurytoma gigantea*. This wasp is also capable of chewing its way out of the gall; however, unlike *E. obtusiventris*, it consumes the fly larva early on and then begins feeding on the walls of the gall. Hence the enlarged central chamber and the dark, granular waste material in it. *E. gigantea* winters in the gall as a naked wasp larva.

INQUILINES

If you cut into a gall during the summer and you find a hard-headed grub feeding in the thick walls, you've found one of the gall fly's *inquilines*: a creature that lives in the nest, burrow, or home of another without harming it. (The long-legged spiders, family Pholcidae, that hang upside down in ceiling corners are inquilines of humans.) The grub is probably *Mordellistema unicolor*, a beetle. Unfortunately for the gall fly, *M. unicolor* has something of a Jekyll-and-Hyde character. It's content to feed on plant matter when nothing else is available, but if it accidentally breaks into the central chamber, it turns predaceous and eats its host.

NEW TENANTS, OLD HOUSES

In September, while you're checking the new year's crop of ball galls, collect twenty of last year's. If possible, take ten from old stems that are still standing and ten from old stems that are lying on the ground. If you live in an area that has heavy snows, standing stems may be hard to find. Look for them at the bases of shrubs and in brushy fields where the herbaceous goldenrod stems are supported by the stronger stems of woody plants.

Spread the twenty old galls on a table and examine each one. You'll find that most of them fall into one of six categories: (1) gall intact, no exit hole, or exit hole less than one-sixteenth of an inch in diameter, (2) gall with a round hole one-eighth of an inch in diameter, (3) gall with a hole plugged with soil, (4) gall with a hole plugged with a clear, parchmentlike material, (5) gall with a large, irregular, tapered hole leading directly to the central chamber, and (6) gall chewed open (Figure 7-4). What do these signs mean?

A gall with no exit hole, or with a very small one, indicates that the larva either died of natural causes or was parasitized, perhaps by one of the two small wasps mentioned above. Cut it open and try to deduce what happened.

Things went well for the larva if a gall has a hole in it one-eighth of an inch in diameter. Cut such a gall open and you'll see a hallway leading from the exit hole to the central chamber and an

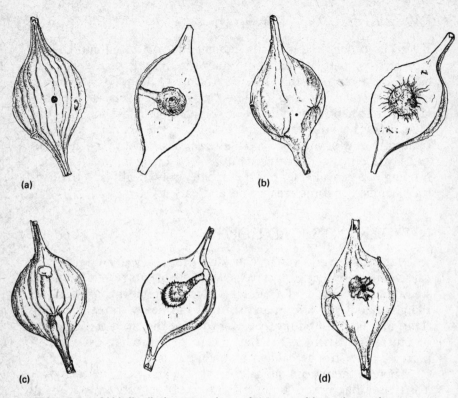

FIGURE 7-4. Old ball galls showing evidence of: (a) successful completion of pupation; (b) parasitism; (c) secondary occupancy; and (d) downy woodpecker predation.

opened pupal case therein. Cut into the gall gently; someone else may be at home. Like our own stout houses, vacated galls don't stay empty for long. Small beetles, earwigs, and other insects often move in. If you tap a gall several times before opening it, the new tenant may stick its head out to see what's going on.

Occasionally you'll find a gall with an exit hole artfully plugged with soil. This indicates that the gall is occupied by one of the small (about a quarter of an inch) solitary wasps (family Vespidae). An adult solitary wasp laid an egg in the vacated gall, provisioned the egg with several caterpillars (some species use spiders), then sealed the opening with a mud plug. Upon hatching, the wasp larva will feed on the caterpillars, winter as a larva, pupate in spring, and then emerge as an adult. The wasp larva is white, as is the gall fly larva, but you can recognize it by its pointed posterior end, large, easily counted segments, and brown jaws.

A gall with a clear, parchmentlike plug over the exit hole is occupied by another artisan: one of the solitary bees (family Colletidae). Unlike the wasp, the adult bee provisions its larvae with pollen rather than caterpillars.

A gall with an irregular, tapered hole leading to the central chamber indicates that a downy woodpecker (*Dendrocopos pubescens*) has been by. Downies have learned to seek out gall fly larvae during the lean times of winter. They are very thorough, and in the spring you may find fields in which over 50 percent of the galls have been breached by downies.

A gall that has been chewed open indicates the work of a small mammal, most likely a rodent of some sort. These galls are relatively rare. Small mammals may find that the food value of the larvae is worth less than the energy required to get at them. Try opening a dry gall with your teeth.

Some of the old galls you find won't fit any of the above descriptions. You may be able to identify the causal agents in these cases on your own, but when an unknown insect is involved, especially as a larva, identification becomes difficult. If one of your unknowns occurs again and again, you may want to take several specimens, galls and all, to an entomologist at a nearby college or agricultural experiment station for identification.

ELLIPTICAL GALLS

If ball galls are houses, elliptical galls are mansions. Not only are they larger, 2 to 3 inches long as opposed to 1½ inches, but in August a hole fitted with a tiny door appears at the top of each gall (Figure 7-5). Even though the door is too high, there is something of the tepee's beauty in the elliptical gall's elegantly tapered top. Add to this both the reddish blush that "ripe" elliptical galls acquire and their relative rarity, and you have a woodland bijou worth searching for.

Elliptical galls occur on Canada goldenrod as well as on sever-

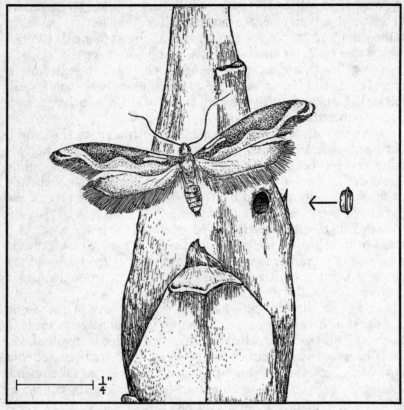

FIGURE 7-5. Elliptical gall and elliptical gall moth.

al closely related species. Look for them closer to the ground than ball galls, usually on the lower half of the stem. They're likely to be found on isolated clones and plants bordering old fields. If you look for them in high, dense clones, "swim" through the clones: stick your arms straight out in front of you, then stroke them back to your sides. Repeat this maneuver as you move forward and it will expose stems. Elliptical galls often disrupt normal growth patterns, so check for them on Canada goldenrods that have three or four main branches rather than a single stem.

THE ELLIPTICAL GALL MOTH

When you find an elliptical gall, examine its dome; if it is after July, you may see a round hole in the top of it. If there is no door covering the hole, or if the door is open and swinging on a "hinge," the occupant is out and will not be back. If the door is shut, the occupant is in.

In early August, collect an elliptical gall with a closed door, plant and all. Cut the goldenrod close to the ground and place it in a soda bottle filled with water. Keep the bottle outside in a protected area. If you keep it in the house, changes in temperature and humidity might disrupt the metamorphosis going on inside. Assuming all goes well, within several days or weeks a small, bedraggled moth (*Gnorimoshema gallaesolidaginus*) will creep out the door, rest awhile as its wings expand and harden, and then fly away.

You can detain the moth long enough to get a good look at it by building a cage around the gall. Remove any leaves or branches on or close to the gall and cut a 6- by 10-inch piece of window screen; either aluminum or nylon screen will do. Hold the screen with the 10-inch axis horizontal and fold it in half around the gall. Staple the three open edges of this cage together and seal them with electrical tape; then press the ends of the cage in just enough to push the sides outward. This will give the moth roomier quarters. After the moth has emerged and you've examined it, release it in a field of goldenrods so that it can carry on its mothy business.

Like others of its kind, the elliptical gall moth you release will mate in late summer. After mating, the females deposit their eggs on rhizomes of Canada goldenrods and other closely related species. The eggs are placed on buds that will become next year's stems. Shortly thereafter the adults die, leaving the wisdom of their race packed away in winterproof eggs.

The following spring, when the new goldenrod stems are shin high, caterpillars (moth larvae) approximately one-eighth of an inch long emerge from the eggs. Each caterpillar immediately bores down into the soft, young tissue at the tip of the stem and on into the more mature tissue below. Once mature tissue is reached, the tiny caterpillar backs up to the region of growing tissue and begins excavating a 2- to 3-inch chamber in the center of the stem. This curious backup maneuver ensures that the caterpillar begins construction in a region of the stem that is mature enough to withstand excavation, but young enough to undergo the deformation that produces an elliptical gall. Evidently, the caterpillar is equipped with directions for finding tissue of the appropriate age, but the directions are of the turn-around-you-just-passed-it variety.

As the caterpillar removes a section of pith to create its central chamber, the walls of the stem around the chamber thicken, expand, and harden to form an elliptical gall. Just before the walls harden, the caterpillar excavates an exit tunnel near the top of the dome. But it, too, stops short of breaking through to the outside, leaving the stem's outer layer of cells in place as a temporary door. The caterpillar then settles down for a summer of uninterrupted feeding.

A succulent layer of cells grows on the gall's inner walls, and the strong-jawed caterpillar feeds on them by systematically scouring the walls with a swaying motion of its head, much like a cow feeding in lush pasture. The caterpillar's solid waste, or *frass*, falls to the bottom of the hold, and the caterpillar occasionally packs it down into the old "backup burrow." Mold, which might readily form on the frass, is kept in check by the flow of an antiseptic goldenrod resin called *solidagin*. In all, the caterpillar enjoys a pleasant summer swaying above the meadow in the green glow of its moist chamber.

Toward the middle of July or early August, the goldenrod is relatively mature, and the walls of the gall stop producing edible cells. This frees the caterpillar for pupation. If it had stopped eating previous to this time, the caterpillar would have been crushed by ingrowing walls.

Before pupating, the caterpillar removes the temporary exit door and crafts a door jamb by reaming the outer edge of the exit hole to create a shoulder. It then spins a thick, round door called an *operculum*, which fits the jamb perfectly. This jamb is constructed so as to prevent the door from being pushed in from the outside. (Has the door to your own home been so prudently designed?) A hand lens will help you appreciate this piece of craftsmanship.

After completing the door, the caterpillar lines the inside of the gall with silk, spins a cocoon, and begins to pupate. In approximately four weeks, sometime from the middle of August to early September, a moth emerges from the cocoon, pushes the door open, and steps outside. Mating begins shortly thereafter, and the cycle goes on.

Used elliptical galls are not as durable as used ball galls and they're harder to find. But if you do find one, slice it open lengthwise and you may find either the empty cocoon or signs of parasitism, predation, or secondary occupancy, just as you did when looking into used ball galls. Slice the stem above and below the gall in half as well and you'll see evidence of the caterpillar's early burrowing, including the backup burrow directly below the hold.

SCARRED GALLS

Scarred goldenrod galls are humbler in appearance than either ball galls or elliptical galls, but they're more "active." The caterpillar inside will throw out the trash and make home repairs while you watch.

Scarred galls are found on a variety of goldenrods, including the Canada goldenrod. They often occur high on the plant, and may even be found on flowering branches. Look for irregular swellings, approximately 1 inch long and three-eighths of an inch wide, with perpendicular brown furrows or *scars* (Figure 7-6). Generally, scarred galls are less numerous than ball galls, but more numerous than elliptical galls. Once you find your first one, you should have no problem finding others. If you do, look for goldenrods with stunted tops. Unlike ball galls and elliptical galls, scarred galls seriously disrupt the flow of fluids within stems, thus limiting growth above the points at which they occur.

When you find a scarred gall in late summer, collect it—plant and all—and put the plant in a soda bottle filled with water. Keep the plant on your desk for a day or two and see what happens. If granular, sawdustlike particles appear on the desk or on the leaves below the gall, all is well with the caterpillar (*Eucosma scudderiana*) inside. Trace the granular particles back to the gall and you'll see a small hole covered with a black silk screen. It's the back door, and the caterpillar uses it to dispose of frass.

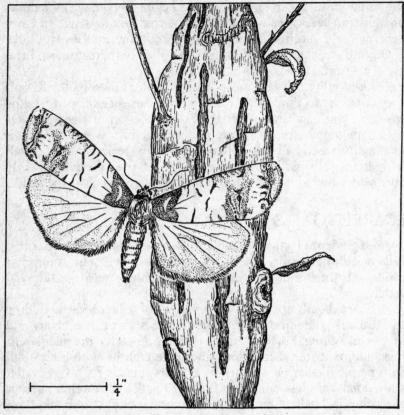

FIGURE 7-6. Scarred gall and scarred gall moth.

If you want to see the caterpillar in action as a house carpenter, cut away a section of the dome. Make a perpendicular cut into the top of the dome about a quarter of an inch deep; then make a horizontal cut into the face of the dome to meet the lower edge of the first cut. This will create a semicircular opening in the central chamber. While you're at work destroying its roof, the caterpillar inside will retreat to the hold. But shortly after your job is done, the caterpillar's head will appear at the opening. After surveying the damage, the caterpillar will begin weaving a silken patch to repair the hole, and in less than fifteen minutes the roof will be sealed tight. Stick the goldenrod, gall and all, in the ground where you found it, and the caterpillar may survive the winter.

Before settling down for its winter rest, the caterpillar excavates an exit door in the dome. This door is difficult to locate because the caterpillar stops short of breaking through the gall, leaving the door sealed by the goldenrod's outer layer of cells. A chamber in the stem just below the hold is also excavated. Here the caterpillar spins a fluffy sack—not a cocoon because it doesn't pupate in it—in which to spend the winter. Like the goldenrod gall fly larva, the scarred gall moth caterpillar also shrinks in size as it loses water in preparation for the freezing temperatures of winter.

Dormancy lasts until May, when the caterpillar creeps out of the sack and into the dome where it positions itself near the exit door. Here it forms a pupa and the six-week pupation period begins. By mid-June, the pupation period is over and the moth's head and legs break through the pupal case. Half in and half out of the case, the moth drags itself to the now-weathered door and breaks through to the outside. As the moth clambers out the door, the pupal case becomes jammed in the doorway, allowing the moth to leave the case behind.

Once out of their galls, the adult moths mate and the females lay their eggs on goldenrod stems, which in June are about knee high. Eggs are often placed where leaves or branches join the stem. When an egg hatches, the larva bores into the side of the stem and begins to excavate a central chamber at the point of entry. The entrance hole becomes the "back door." In excavating the central chamber, the larva chews away much of the conducting tissue in the dome, and the thin, weakened dome serves as a ventilator for the active caterpillar inside. Feeding takes place in the hold where the walls of the stem have not been chewed away. When the goldenrod stops growing in late August or September, the caterpillar begins making preparations for winter.

The scarred gall caterpillar is subject to the same sorts of parasites and predators that attack the other gall-makers. But since scarred galls are weaker structurally than ball galls and elliptical galls, they usually don't last long enough to shelter second owners.

OTHER GOLDENROD GALLS

Goldenrods are subject to well over fifty other galls that occur on leaves, roots, and flowers, as well as stems, and not all of them appear as swellings. As you meander through the goldenrods, you'll see tight bunches of leaves, similar to little artichokes, on some of the plants. These are *rosette*, or *bunch galls*, and they're caused by small flies called *midges*. The black, raised spots you see on the leaves of the grass-leaved goldenrod are *blister galls*, and they, too, are caused by a midge. Midges also cause galls on individual goldenrod flowers, which make the flowers look long and hairy.

Conclusion

The Canada goldenrod is commonplace—the *vin ordinaire* of North American wildflowers—but it is a rich and complex wine nonetheless and well worthy of your full attention. *Salud Solidago!*

Thought Questions

1. In an early study of goldenrod galls, it was noted that the doors on elliptical galls often face north, but rarely south. What explanation can you offer for this phenomenon?

   Hint: In framing an answer, the researcher who conducted the study assumed that a moth larva inside an elliptical gall would choose the path of least resistance when excavating a door. He also assumed that the side of the gall that received the least sunlight would have comparatively soft, moist walls. By the way, *do* the doors really face north more often than south?

2. Studies have shown that the Canada goldenrod produces compounds that harm sugar maple seedlings and reduce the germination of many plant seeds. How might these compounds serve the Canada goldenrod?

   Hint: When a farm is abandoned in eastern North America, it reverts back to woods through a gradual process known as *plant succession.* Grasses and weeds arrive first, but they are soon crowded out and shaded out by fast-growing, sun-loving shrubs and trees such as aspens, willows, and cherries. These in turn are replaced by slow-growing but shade-tolerant species such as maples, hickories, and beech. In many areas a field can go from corn to maples in thirty years; however, the process of succession is apt to take longer in fields that are invaded early on by Canada goldenrod. In fact, some old-timers in New York and New England speak of the goldenrod's ability to "hold" a field.

3. In your search for galls, you may have noticed herds of treehoppers, small insects in the family Membracidae, tended by ants. The treehoppers suck the goldenrod's sap, and the ants "milk" the treehoppers for *insect nectar.* One might think that these herds and herders would have adverse effects on goldenrods. But under certain conditions the opposite is true. Goldenrods with treehoppers and ants grow taller and produce more seeds than nearby goldenrods without them. Explain.

Hint: The relationship between the treehoppers and the ants is *mutualistic,* each benefits. The ants obtain food from the treehoppers, and in return they chase away herbivorous insects, such as leaf-eating striped goldenrod beetles, that might otherwise take over the treehoppers' feeding grounds. Since a bit of sap is a far less serious loss than many leaves, entomologists say that the Canada goldenrod has an "indirect mutualistic relationship" with treehoppers and ants.

4. Sometime in July, saw a 12- × 1- × 1-inch strip of wood into four 3-inch sections. Then drill three evenly spaced holes, half an inch deep and three-sixteenths of an inch in diameter, in one face of each piece. Each hole must have a solid bottom. Tie three of the pieces to sticks from 1 to 3 feet high and set them up like bird houses in protected places, with southern exposures, along the edges of a field of goldenrods. Place the fourth piece on your window sill, holes up. With a little luck, what will the holes attract?

Hint: The solitary wasps and bees that use old ball galls as nests are not committed to them; any sound hole will do.

5. Curious naturalists and hungry downy woodpeckers aren't the only ones who seek ball galls in winter. Some ice fishermen do too. Why?

Hint: These ice fishermen are usually angling for small bait fish or for small, edible fish, such as perch and smelt.

Recommended Reading

BORROR, DONALD J. and WHITE, RICHARD E. *A Field Guide to the Insects of America North of Mexico.* Boston: Houghton Mifflin Co., 1970. A field guide to insect families. Excellent drawings and a good introduction to collecting and understanding insects.

COMSTOCK, JOHN HENRY and COMSTOCK, ANNA BOTSFORD. *A Manual for the Study of Insects.* Ithaca, New York: Comstock Publishing Co., 1897. After you've identified an insect with one of the contemporary field guides and you want to know more about it, this is the book to turn to. The Comstocks are a pleasure to read, and they tell you what you want to know about insects: where to find them, what they eat, and how they reproduce. (Thirty years after its publication, J. H. Comstock revised the *Manual,* and the revision was published as *An Introduction to Entomology.*)

FELT, EPHRAIM PORTER. *Plant Galls and Gall Makers.* Ithaca, New York: Comstock Publishing Co., 1940. The best guide available for the identification of North American galls. Excellent illustrations and photographs make it easy to use. The introduction contains an overview of galls and gall-makers.

HUTCHINS, ROSS E. *Galls and Gall Insects.* New York: Dodd, Mead and Co., 1969. A nontechnical introduction to galls and gall insects. Superb photographs of the life cycles of the ball gall fly and the elliptical gall moth and an interesting chapter on the history and importance of galls. Intended for young readers, but adults will enjoy it too.

STOKES, DONALD W. *A Guide to Nature in Winter.* Boston: Little, Brown and Co., 1976. A good introduction to the Northeastern and North Central woods in winter, with a fourteen-page section on galls.

WERNER, PATRICIA A., BADBURG, IAN K., and GROSS, RONALD S. "The Biology of Canada Weeds. 45. *Solidago canadensis L."* *Canadian Journal of Plant Sciences.* Vol. 60. October 1980, pp. 1393–1409. This paper is worth a trip to a college library. In addition to a wealth of information on the Canada goldenrod, it contains an extensive bibliography.

CHAPTER EIGHT
Trees

The mortal who has never enjoyed a speaking acquaintance with some individual tree is to be pitied; for such an acquaintance, once established, naturally ripens into a friendliness that brings serene comfort to the human heart, whatever the heart of the tree may or may not experience. To those who know them, the trees, like other friends, seem to have their periods of reaching out for sympathetic understanding. How often this outreaching is met with repulse will never be told; for tree friends never reproach us,—but wait with calm patience for us to grow into comprehension.

Anna Botsford Comstock
Trees at Leisure, 1916

Trees are the great fact of eastern North America, and the satisfaction that you obtain out-of-doors will increase in direct proportion to your ability to appreciate them. The classic approach is to deal with trees as *personalities*: learn to recognize and enjoy the distinctive pattern of characteristics that distinguishes each species from all others. This approach requires prolonged contact under a variety of circumstances, because like other living things, trees can't reveal themselves all at once. However, you can get an initial impression of a tree's personality, and thereby make a "speaking acquaintance" of it, by doing the following three things: (1) find out what the species' common names are, (2) learn how to recognize the species at a glance, and (3) visit the biggest member of the species you can find.

Tree Names

COMMON

In the woods we are all *taxonomists* (scientists who classify and name organisms), and the fundamental question is: What's it called? In addition to satisfying this basic curiosity, tree names are worth knowing both for what they are and for what they do. Many names, such as "hackmatack," "catalpa," and "oak," are a pleasure to say and to hear. Others, such as "sugar maple," "lodgepole pine," and "Kentucky coffeetree," tell something about the relationships people have had with the trees named. Finally, names serve as handles that help us get mental holds on new acquaintances. So whether you're dealing with people or plants, it's important to get names straight at the outset.

Most trees have several common names that vary according to region, period in history when named, and the occupation of the namer. The tuliptree, for example, is called "tuliptree" by those who know it as a shade and ornamental tree; they admire the showy, tuliplike flowers that appear on the tree in April and May (Figure 8-1). Country folk call it the "tulip poplar" or "popple"; they know that like the true poplars, its wood is soft and easily worked. Children who know what horses are for call it the "saddle-

FIGURE 8-1. The tuliptree (*Liriodendron tulipifera*).

leaf," because of the pronounced notch at the top of each of its leaves. Loggers know it as the "yellow poplar"; when they fell the tree they expose its yellow heartwood. The architects and carpenters of early New England appreciated the tulip's creamy-white sapwood, and so called it "whitewood." Those mindful of North American history call it "canoewood," because Indians and settlers found its long, straight trunks ideal for building dugout canoes. The Onondaga Indians called it "Ko-yen-ta-ka-ah-tas," or "white tree." They may have been impressed by the white inner color of its twigs and branches or by the way the tuliptree plays with light by flashing it off the silver undersides of its leaves. What's in a name? Plenty.

If you know one common name for a species, you can find out if it has any others by looking it up in one of the books listed under Recommended Reading. Common names, however, are just that, so check for more with farmers, loggers, and other residents of the area in which the species grows. When you meet a tree that you don't know by any name, use a field guide to identify it.

SCIENTIFIC

Despite their value, common names can be confusing. Depending on where you are and who you're talking with, "whitewood" may be used to refer to the tuliptree, the basswood, or the eastern cottonwood. Fortunately, each species has a *scientific name* as well as common names, and there is only one scientific name for each species. That name is determined in accordance with the International Code of Botanical Nomenclature, so when you refer to a tree by its scientific name, knowledgeable people the world over will know what tree you're talking about.

The tuliptree's scientific name is *Liriodendron tulipifera* (*Liriodendron* is derived from the Greek term for "lilylike flower"). If you know plant taxonomy, a tree's scientific name is the key to understanding its phylogenetic relationships (family relationships and evolutionary history), but even if you don't know anything about taxonomy, scientific names are worth learning. In addition to eliminating confusion, they can be used in casual conversation to annoy your friends, and some are simply fun to pronounce. For example,

once you know that the box elder's scientific name is _Acer negundo,_
why would you call it anything else?

Recognizing Trees

After having identified a tree with the aid of a field guide, you'll
probably be able to identify other members of the same species by
carefully looking for the trenchant characteristics denoted in the
guide. That's a start, but you won't get to know a tree's personality
that way. If you have to _identify_ each species every time you see it,
trees will frustrate and bore you. In order to start enjoying trees on a
first-name basis, you have to go beyond identification to _immediate
recognition_—the kind of thing that occurs when you recognize a
friend glimpsed in a crowd. This is done by learning the pattern, or
gestalt, that gives each species away.

A gestalt is formed by two or more characteristics, but it is
more than the mere sum of those characteristics; it's a unified
whole. For example, think of a close friend that you can recognize
at a glance. How do you do it? Shape of chin? Eye color? Posture?
Dress? Without some thought and a close look at the friend in
question, you may not be able to tell how you do it. Your ability to
recognize a friend is probably not based on one or two individual
features, but rather on the total impression made by a number of
features. Recognizing a tree occurs in the same way.

Glance at the two drawings in Figure 8-2. They represent the
gestalts of two common trees. Recognize either of them? Drawing
"a" represents the catalpa (_Catalpa speciosa_), or Indian bean tree.
The scraggly, horizontal lines are branches, and the slightly bowed,
vertical lines are the persistent, beanlike fruits. Other trees have
branches and beanlike fruits, but none come together to form a
gestalt like the catalpa's. Drawing "b" represents the honeylocust
(_Gleditsia tricanthos_). The long, hard thorns on the trunk and lower
branches are distinctive, but you're only _identifying_ the honeylocust
if you have to walk up to it, examine the thorns, and think,
"Hmm, hard, sharp, branched thorns approximately 2 to 3 inches
long—must be a honeylocust." You're _recognizing_ it when you see

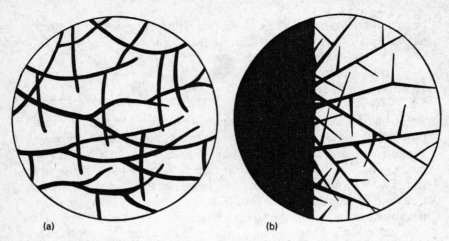

(a)   (b)

FIGURE 8-2. Gestalts of two common trees: (a) catalpa (*Catalpa speciosa*); and (b) honeylocust (*Gleditsia triacanthos*).

irregular masses on a dark column in the distance and your mind flashes—honeylocust!

One of the most telling physical characteristics of a tree is its general shape, or branching pattern. Even at a distance of a mile or more, it's easy to differentiate between the compact, oval *crown* (the leaf-bearing portion of a tree above the lower trunk) of an open-grown sugar maple (*Acer saccharum*) and the spreading, vase-shaped crown of an open-grown American elm (*Ulmus americana*). Of course, in dense forests, where individual trees must compete for growing room and sunlight, they are not as free to express themselves, so they generally develop long, straight trunks and limited crowns. Therefore, it's important to visit both *open-grown* and *forest-grown* specimens when familiarizing yourself with a species (Figure 8-3).

Gestalts change with seasons as well as with growing conditions. In summer, noisy leaves help to give the quaking aspen (*Populus tremuloides*) away, but in winter you have to rely on its yellow-green bark, central stem, and sunny location. With practice you'll find that winter is actually the best time to learn to recognize *deciduous trees* (trees that lose all of their leaves at the end of the growing season, as opposed to *evergreen trees*). Leaves are like

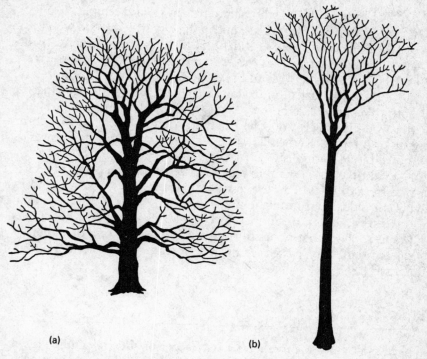

(a)   (b)

FIGURE 8-3. An (a) open-grown and (b) forest-grown American beech (*Fagus grandifolia*) in winter.

a uniform: If you don't know a species well, they may help you to identify it, but once you're on familiar terms with a species, you'll find it easier to recognize when it stands naked and innocent before you.

In addition to such characteristics as branching pattern, bark texture, and the response of leaves to the wind, contextual cues may play a part in forming a tree's gestalt. Some species are normally associated with certain soil conditions, geographic locations, specific cultural and economic activities, and/or particular plants and animals. Black willows (*Salix niger*) like their feet wet, so you'll find them bordering lowland streams rather than in dry uplands. Ginkgoes (*Ginkgo balboa*) have never been found growing in the wild (they may have been saved from extinction hundreds of years ago by Oriental monks who planted them around temples), so look for them in parks, front yards, and along city streets. And when you see the Baltimore oriole's pendant nest, think of the American elm and the silver maple (*Acer saccharinum*), because these are the trees in which the oriole likes to build.

Once you learn to recognize a species, use words, drawings or both to make a record of its gestalt in your field notebook. Gestalts that you intuitively know best may be the most difficult to record. But keep trying. Knowing how you know is your source of power as a qualitative naturalist.

In time your own skill may surprise you as you begin to recognize trees in televised newscasts, in magazine photographs, and in distant fields seen from the corner of your eye as you cruise along the interstate. Thoreau once recognized several large white pines (*Pinus strobus*) that he used to visit in the woods of a neighboring town when they passed through Concord as logs on a railroad flatcar!

Big Trees

You can't fully comprehend a tree's personality, assuming it's a long-lived species, until you've seen what it will become after centuries of growth. (As Thoreau said, "I fear that the rising generation in this town do not know what an oak or a pine is, having seen only inferior specimens.") Your concept of the white pine will expand after you've looked up at smooth, massive columns converging toward a point 150 feet above your head; and you'll understand what sycamores (*Platanus occidentalis*) are about after you've taken the long walk around one with a trunk 6 feet in diameter. Patriarchs like these are still around. Some are relics of the primeval forest that now find themselves standing alone between parking lots and highways; others continue to grow on small tracts that have never been logged; and some are old second-growth trees.

The quickest way to locate big trees is with the aid of an expert. Your state forester's office or state forestry commission should be able to provide you with the names, locations, and measurements of the biggest trees in your state, and your county forester or cooperative extension forester will be able to direct you to some of the big trees near your home. For a nominal fee, The American Forestry Association will send you a copy of the "National Register of Big Trees" (see Recommended Reading), which consists of a partially illustrated list of the biggest trees in the United States. When searching for big trees on your own, check front lawns in old neighborhoods, college campuses, and cemeteries, as well as the woods.

MEASURING

Measuring a big tree may sound almost sacrilegious, but if you do it in the proper spirit, you'll understand why Oliver Wendell Holmes referred to his tape measure as a "wedding band" and to the trees he wrapped it around as his "tree wives." Measuring a tree is an intimate and revealing act.

Diameter breast high, or d.b.h., is the measurement most often taken by foresters, and it's almost always included in official records. If you use it, you'll be able to compare your records with other records. Diameter breast high is determined as follows:

1. Use a tape to measure the circumference of the tree at 4.5 feet above the ground.
2. Divide the circumference by π (approximately 3.14). The quotient is equal to the tree's d.b.h.

Got it? What's the d.b.h. of a white oak (_Quercus alba_) with a circumference of 16 feet, 7 inches at 4.5 feet above ground? Before you begin, remember that when measuring a tree, pinpoint accuracy is as inappropriate as it is when measuring a growing child, so feel free to round off in favor of the growing tree. Calculations will go easier if you work in inches, then convert back to feet and inches when you have the answer.

The d.b.h. of the white oak in our example is 5 feet, 4 inches. That's a big white oak. (The largest living white oak on record is in a state park in Wye Mills, Maryland. In 1972 it had a d.b.h. of 9 feet, 4 inches.) Always attach dates to your d.b.h. measurements; like people, trees increase in diameter with age.

Height. There are several ways to determine the approximate height of a tree without climbing it or cutting it down. One of the most convenient and least expensive methods is to use a homemade version of a device foresters call a *Biltmore stick.*

When you come across a tree and want to know its height, find yourself a straight stick about 4 feet long and an inch or so in diameter. Walk away from the tree you wish to measure until you're standing about as far from it as you guess it to be tall. Then position yourself so that you can see both its highest point and its base.

Once situated, hold your arm (left or right) comfortably outstretched in front of you and make an upright vee with your thumb and forefinger. Place the stick in the vee with the heavier end (root end) away from you and with the lighter end (leaf end) just touching your cheekbone, right below your eye.

With your arm outstretched, grasp the stick with your fist and bring the stick into a vertical position. (If you have a stick with a pronounced taper, the extra weight at the root end will cause it to swing into a vertical position almost automatically.) Once the stick is vertical, the distance from the top of your fist to the top of the stick should equal the distance from your eye to the top of your fist. This is an essential relationship and it must be maintained.

With the stick in its vertical position, sight the base of the tree over your fist. If you find it necessary to move your arm up or down to do this, adjust the length of the stick above your fist so that it once again equals the distance from your eye to your fist. This is easily accomplished by tilting the stick back to your cheekbone while holding your arm in the new position.

Now, without moving your head, cast your eyes to the top of the stick and walk toward or away from the tree until the top of the stick is even with the top of the tree. When (1) the top of the stick is even with the top of the tree, and (2) the top of your fist is even with the base of the tree, and (3) the length of the stick above your fist is equal to the distance from the top of your fist to your eye, mark the spot you're standing on. The distance from that spot to the base of the tree is a fair approximation of the tree's height.

Foresters claim that with a little practice this method will produce results within 5 percent of a tree's actual height, and with a lot of practice it will produce results within 1 percent of the actual

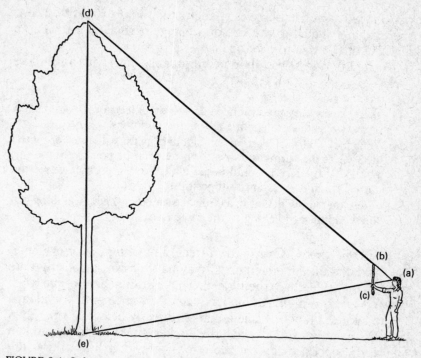

FIGURE 8-4. Sighting a tree when estimating its height with a homemade Biltmore stick. Note that the large triangle *ade* is similar to the smaller triangle *abc*, and that lines *ed* and *ea*, and lines *cb* and *ca*, are equal length sides of similar isosceles triangles.

height. As you may recall from your study of trigonometry, this method is based on the *principle of similar triangles*. All your sighting and moving around is an attempt to create two *similar isosceles triangles* (triangles with two sides of equal length, whose corresponding sides are proportional). One is a larger triangle whose two equal sides meet at the tree's base, and extend, respectively, to the top of the tree and to your eye. The other is a smaller triangle whose two equal sides meet at your fist, and extend, respectively, to the top of the stick and to your eye (Figure 8-4). You can get an approximation of the length of the side of the large triangle that runs from your eye to the base of the tree by measuring the distance from where you were standing to the base of the tree. Since you were working with similar isosceles triangles, you know that distance is approximately equal to the side of the large triangle that runs from the base of the tree to the top.

The following tips will increase your accuracy with a Biltmore stick:

1. Before measuring trees, hone your skill on objects of known height, such as flagpoles, telephone poles, and buildings.
2. Your stick will work best on level ground, but it will also work if the tree you're measuring is downhill. It may not be possible to use this method if the tree is uphill because it's often impossible to see the top of a tree from a downhill position.
3. When measuring height in a forest, be sure that the base and top you are working with belong to the same tree.

Crown Spread. Open-grown trees of some types (for example, oaks and certain American elms) may have crown spreads that are more impressive than their heights. You can measure *maximum crown spread* by walking around a tree at a distance until you identify the longest branch. Place a marker directly below its tip. Then draw an imaginary line through the marker, the tree's trunk, and on out to the opposite edge of the crown. Use that line to find the branch tip opposite the longest branch and place another marker directly below it. Measure the distance between the two markers and you should have the maximum crown spread. (But measure a few more sets of opposite branch tips just to be sure.) Use the same technique to find the crown's smallest diameter and you'll have the *minimum crown spread.* If you want to determine the *average crown spread,* a measurement used in some record books, add the maximum and minimum crown spreads and divide by two. All crown spread measurements are usually taken to only the nearest foot.

Conclusion

There's a sycamore in the little town of Sunderland, Massachusetts, that is said to be well over 500 years old, yet each spring it puts forth new leaves as fresh as those it bore when Indian moccasins tamped its roots. The tree stands between a sidewalk and a residential street, and if you drive from the hills of Amherst to see it, you'll spot its massive crown from miles away as you drop into the Connecticut River Valley. That sycamore was a big tree before the house in front of which it stands was built, before the road that it shades was laid out, and before towns such as Sunderland, Amherst, and Boston were founded. Nevertheless, no obvious precautions have been taken to safeguard the tree, and no festival is held in its honor. We have a great deal to learn about appreciating trees.

Thought Questions

1. It's been said that the fastest way to make friends with someone is to ask him or her to do something for you—something he or she does well. How might you apply this to trees?

Hint: One way to get to know a tree is by putting some part of it to use. Harvest fruits of the black walnut (*Juglans nigra*) and use them in a cookie recipe; no other nut will fill your kitchen with so fruity an aroma. Replace the plastic handles on your jackknife with pieces of flowering dogwood (*Cornus florida*); it will take a higher luster and resist splintering better than any other eastern hardwood. Or make a painter, or bow line, for your canoe from retted basswood (*Tilia americana*) bark; when wet it beats other natural fibers for handling (for directions see Harlow's *Ways of the Woods*, listed in Recommended Reading, Chapter 2). Your relationship with a tree will change for the better after you've used some part of it wisely.

2. What species of tree has been appreciated above all others by citizens of the United States?

Hint: The Liberty Tree was a member of this species, and it was the first tree that Yankees took from the primeval forest and planted alongside their homes. Before an alien disease struck it, this species was widely planted as a street tree by towns across the nation, and it still remains the tree of choice on college campuses. The eighteenth-century botanist André Michaux dubbed it "the most magnificent vegetable of the temperate zone," and Donald Culross Peattie (see Recommended Reading) called it a "fountain of vegetation." Its scientific name is *Ulmus americana*.

3. What evergreen tree is said to have been the first North American tree introduced into Europe?

Hint: One of its common names means "tree of life," an honorific title bestowed on it by sailors who were saved from "distemper" by drinking a decoction made from its leaves. Today New England farmers use its trunks for long-lasting fence posts, and suburbanites plant it as an ornamental shrub. Its scientific name is *Thuja occidentalis*.

4. You know that the age of a tree can be determined by counting the annual rings on its stump, but do you know what causes the rings?

Hint: Annual rings are composed of water-carrying cells. Each annual ring has two parts, a wide *earlywood* layer composed of large cells that are produced during spring and early summer when moisture is plentiful and growing conditions are ideal, and a narrower *latewood* layer composed of smaller cells produced in late summer when conditions are generally drier and less conducive to rapid growth. (Cells are not produced in winter when trees are dormant.) The densely packed latewood layers are darker in color than the earlywood layers on either side of them, and so produce the rings that people count to determine a tree's age.

5. How can you determine the age of a young white pine without counting its annual rings?

Hint: White pines usually produce one new whorl of branches each year. Depending on growing conditions, these *annual whorls* are spaced from 1 to 2 feet apart. If you're dealing with a healthy tree with a single stem, all you have to do is count the number of whorls from bottom to top, and you'll have a fair approximation of its age. This method works with pines as well as with spruces and firs. It won't work on old, forest-grown trees, because the branches of their lower whorls eventually fall off, and in time all traces of the whorls are covered by new wood and bark.

Recommended Reading

FIELD GUIDES

HARLOW, WILLIAM M. *Trees of the Eastern United States and Canada*. New York: Dover Publications, Inc., 1957. This is the tree book to start with. In the introduction, Dr. Harlow presents a short course on tree anatomy, and he explains how to use a dichotomous key. (A *key* is a printed device used to identify unknown objects; a *dichotomous key* is based on a series of paired choices. By choosing the correct one at each step of the way, the user is led to the name of the object.) The natural history of each species is discussed and there are photographs of trenchant characteristics.

————. *Fruit Key and Twig Key to Trees and Shrubs*. New York: Dover Publications, Inc., 1946. This book is handy in fall, winter, and spring, when deciduous trees don't have leaves.

SYMONDS, GEORGE W. D. *The Tree Identification Book*. New York: William Morrow & Co., 1958. This is a pictorial key and *the* book on tree recognition. Symonds' goal is to help you know trees at a glance. The approach is unique and the photographs are excellent. *The Shrub Identification Book* by the same author is also worth having.

NATURAL HISTORY

COLLINGWOOD, G. H., and BUSH, WARREN D. *Knowing Your Trees*. Washington, D.C.: The American Forestry Association, 1979. A good reference book on the trees of North America. Particularly valuable because it provides photographs of an open-grown specimen of each deciduous species, bare and in leaf. The range maps are excellent, and it's also a good source of common names.

PEATTIE, DONALD CULROSS. *A Natural History of Trees of Eastern and Central North America*. Boston: Houghton Mifflin Co., 1966. A collection of essays on trees by a writer who seems to have been on speaking terms with all of them. Peattie offers a classic blend of botany and history. Rich in common names.

APPRECIATION

COMSTOCK, ANNA BOTSFORD. *Trees At Leisure*. Ithaca, New York: Comstock Publishing Co., 1916. This is the source of this chapter's epigraph. It's unlikely that there is, or ever will be, a more beautiful book on trees than this little-known, fifty-five-page gem.

LEOPOLD, ALDO. "Good Oak." *A Sand County Almanac: With Other Essays on Conservation From Round River.* New York: Oxford University Press, 1966. Those who cut their own wood, or would if they could, will enjoy this one.

THOREAU, HENRY DAVID. "Autumnal Tints." *The Natural History Essays.* Edited with an introduction and notes by Robert Sattelmeyer. Salt Lake City, Utah: Peregrine Smith, Inc., 1980. This is a how-to essay on appreciating trees by the master. The sugar maple, scarlet oak, and American elm are discussed in detail.

MEASUREMENTS

AMERICAN FORESTRY ASSOCIATION. "National Register of Big Trees." *American Forests,* April 1978; reprints available from The American Forestry Association, 1319 18th Street, N.W., Washington, D.C. 20036. In addition to the names, locations, and measurements of the biggest trees in the United States, this booklet contains instructions for nominating trees for standing in the National Register of Big Trees. Available at minimal cost.

CHAPTER NINE
The Whippoorwill's Shoes

*I can fancy that it would be a luxury to stand up to one's
chin in some retired swamp a whole summer day, scenting
the wild honeysuckle and bilberry blows, and lulled by the
minstrelsy of gnats and mosquitoes! A day passed
in the society of those Greek sages, such as described
in the Banquet of Xenophon, would not be comparable with
the dry wit of decayed cranberry vines, and the fresh Attic
salt of the moss-beds. Say twelve hours of genial and
familiar converse with the leopard frog; the sun to rise
behind alder and dogwood, and climb buoyantly to his
meridian of two hands' breadth, and finally sink to rest
behind some bold western hummock. . . . Surely one may
as profitably be soaked in the juices of a swamp for one day
as pick his way dryshod over sand. Cold and damp, —are
they not as rich experience as warmth and dryness?*

Henry David Thoreau
*A Week on the Concord
and Merrimack Rivers,* 1849

On your first visit to a wetland similar to Thoreau's "swamp," twenty to thirty minutes spent chin deep will probably do. If the search for carnivorous plants doesn't keep you moving, the cold water will.

The moss beds and cranberry vines that Thoreau mentions indicate that his *swamp* was probably a *bog*. Northeastern swamps are relatively well-drained wetlands rich in plants, animals, and available nutrients. Bogs, on the other hand, are poorly drained wetlands with a limited variety of plants and animals, and few available nutrients. Yet many naturalists consider bogs to be the most intriguing of aquatic communities. In this chapter we'll find out why.

Bog Formation

Most bogs in the eastern Canadian provinces and in the United States from Minnesota to Massachusetts are glacial in origin. When the continental glaciers receded from these areas approximately 10,000 years ago, they left behind landscapes with confused drainage patterns. Poorly drained depressions were created by the scouring action of ice sheets, the blocking of old drainage courses by glacial till, and the melting of barn-size chunks of ice left in glacial deposits. As the ice melted, these depressions filled with water to form ponds and lakes.

Into this barren landscape came northern species of plants and animals that had been forced southward as the glaciers advanced, but that now followed the retreating glaciers northward to their ancestral homes. Bog communities began to form when these refugees invaded poorly drained ponds and lakes along the way.

Plant succession in those bodies of water that were to become bogs followed a common pattern. At first, only aquatic plants grew in the shallows, but as seasons passed, organic deposits accumulated, allowing amphibious sedges and rushes to move in. Their roots and stems created latticework platforms along the shores, which in turn enabled *sphagnum moss* (*Sphagnum spp.*), a bog hallmark, to enter the communities.

Sphagnum moss—a veritable vegetable beaver—alters the

environment to suit itself, and once it invades a poorly drained depression, that depression's future as a bog is set. Growing in combination with sedges and certain other plants, it forms a floating mat capable of extending out over open water. This mat causes profound changes: it insulates the depression like the top of an ice chest; it prevents sunlight from entering and heating the water; and it releases a rain of dead vegetation that settles to the bottom where it forms thick layers of _peat_. (This is the source of the _peat moss_ that you buy in bales and use as a mulch.) Meanwhile, the ion-exchange activity of the living sphagnum moss, coupled with poor drainage, causes an increase in acidity. Soon only a limited variety of organisms can tolerate the cool, dark, acid waters, and the depression becomes a closed community—a bog.

As the surface mat continues to spread and thicken, the layers of peat below, which decompose extremely slowly because of the near aseptic condition of the water, rise to meet it. In time the entire depression may be filled with peat and covered with an unbroken mat. As this occurs, acid-tolerant shrubs and small trees establish themselves just offshore on the older, more substantial sections of the mat. This "forest" advances outward as the mat thickens and may eventually cover the entire surface of the bog. Today bogs exist in various stages of succession, from open-water ponds with narrow bands of sphagnum hugging the shores, to solid beds of peat whose surfaces support 20-foot spruces, firs, and tamaracks all the way across.

Locating a Bog

Bogs of glacial origin are fairly common in eastern Canada and in the northeastern and north-central United States. However, bogs and boglike communities of other origins can be found in the southeastern, Gulf Coast, and northwestern states as well.

The surest way to locate a bog is to contact the botany department of a university in the area you're interested in. Ask for the professor who teaches field botany or plant taxonomy. Nature centers, Audubon Societies, and agricultural extension offices are also good sources of information on local bogs.

If you're in an area where bogs are common, you may be able to locate one yourself by studying topographic maps of the region (Chapter 4). Look for the stylized tussocks that symbolize wetlands. Of course, not all wetlands are bogs, but some of those that are may be indicated by a white area with tussocks, surrounded by a green area with tussocks, which is itself enclosed or almost enclosed by a contour line and surrounded by plain green. The white area with tussocks represents the treeless portion of the bog mat; the green area with tussocks represents the edges of the bog mat where shrubs and small trees have established themselves; the contour line around the whole represents the drop-off point between solid ground and the sphagnum-filled depression; and the plain green represents a soil-based forest surrounding the bog. If a bog has an area of open water, or an *eye*, there will be a patch of blue somewhere in the center of all this.

Bogs, like other natural objects and events, are where you find them, so don't expect every bog to have the features described above. And even if a bog does have these features, don't count on them appearing on your topographic map, especially if the bog is an acre or less in size. Topographic maps are only approximations; they can't and don't show everything, and some of what they do show may not exist when you visit the site. For example, if your map was based on observations made during a period of high water, then a room-size bog that exists for most of the year as a solid mat with no inlet or outlet may be shown as a blue-water pond with streams entering and leaving it. Similarly, you can't rely on the names that appear on maps to distinguish between ponds, swamps, and bogs. Many a Mud Pond and Finnegan's Swamp on the map are bogs in the field.

Exploring a Bog

Soaking chin deep in a bog is a luxury on hot summer days but an ordeal when the weather is colder, so plan your trip accordingly. Sneakers, long pants, and a T-shirt will get you through the brush surrounding the bog. Once you're on the mat, a bathing or birthday suit will do. The following items will also come in handy:

1. two empty jam or peanut butter jars
2. a kitchen baster with the tip cut off so as to leave an opening at least a quarter of an inch in diameter
3. thermometer
4. pH paper

Pack this equipment in a plastic pail and you're ready to go.

When you see a clearing through the trees and brush, you've found your bog. An abrupt transition from a soil-based woods of large trees to a sphagnum-based woods of shrubs and small trees will signal the surface of the bog proper. You may have to step down at this point. As you proceed to the center of the bog, you'll pass through three concentric vegetation zones: *bog woods, bog shrub,* and *bog mat* (Figure 9-1). The bog woods zone is located on the densest layers of peat and sphagnum, the shrub zone grows on less substantial layers, and the bog mat grows on loose, watery peat or floats on water. If your bog has an eye, there will be a fourth, or *open-water,* zone. Depending on the bog, these zones may be clearly defined or barely distinguishable. But whether you're in a glacial bog in the Northeast Kingdom of Vermont or a coastal bog in the Pocosin Wetlands of North Carolina, you'll see *some* of the plants listed in Figure 9-1, so use your natural history library to familiarize yourself with them beforehand.

THE PITCHER PLANT

Your key to understanding the bog community is the *pitcher plant* (*Sarracenia purpurea*), or as it was once known to country children, the *whippoorwill's shoes.* Look for them on the bog mat where their long-stemmed, nodding flowers give their positions away.

When you find a pitcher plant, kneel beside it and look into one of its "pitchers" (Figure 9-2). You'll see a watery fluid composed of rainwater and plant secretions. There may be a dead or dying insect or two bobbing around in there as well. Pitcher plants are carnivorous. They photosynthesize as do other green plants, but they obtain some nutrients from the bodies of their victims.

Carefully insert your baster into one of the pitchers. When the tip touches bottom, squeeze and release the bulb several times

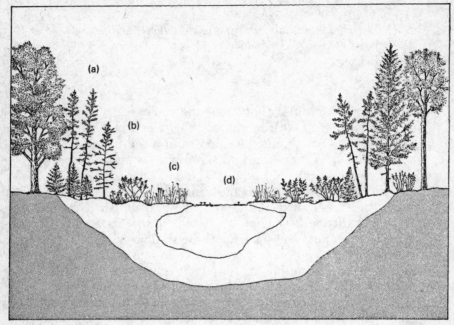

FIGURE 9-1. A cross-section diagram of a northern bog illustrating the four concentric vegetation zones: (a) *bog woods* (balsam fir, black spruce, eastern hemlock, tamarack, red maple, yellow birch); (b) *bog shrub*, (chokeberry, highbush blueberry, highbush cranberry, bog rosemary, leatherleaf, Labrador tea); (c) *bog mat* (sedges, sphagnum moss, buckbean, cotton grass, cranberry, creeping snowberry, pitcher plant [carnivorous], sundew [carnivorous]); (d) *open water* (yellow pond lily).

to stir up the contents of the pitcher. Wait a moment for things to settle, then fill the baster and transfer its contents to a glass jar. When you examine the liquid, you'll find beetle wing covers, wasp heads, fly wings, and other indigestible insect parts. (What's fair is fair, so pour the liquid and its contents back into the pitcher after you've examined it.) Sample a number of pitchers. You'll be surprised at the number of things you come up with. Pitcher plants are not picky eaters.

You may want to take a sample of pitcher fluid home. This mixture is said to contain secretions that immobilize insects faster than plain water, and it also contains digestive enzymes that act on proteins. How might you test for the latter?

Ingenius Traps. A pitcher plant attracts its prey in two ways. The beautifully shaped and colored mouth of each pitcher resembles a flower, and cells on the inner surface of the lower lip release a sweet-smelling nectar. Once an insect lands on the pitcher's mouth, it is led toward the digestive fluid by trails of nectar cells. Each step brings it closer to two more adaptations that may seal its fate. Find out what they are by sliding your finger in and out of a pitcher along its lower lip. Did you feel two different textures? Like many things in life, pitcher plants are easier to get into than out of.

An Inhospitable Habitat. The pitcher plant's carnivorous habit is a response to an inhospitable habitat. Stick your arm into the sphagnum moss and peat below a pitcher plant, and use your thermometer to compare that temperature with the temperature of the air, or with the temperature of a quart or two of water that has been sitting in your bucket in the sun.

FIGURE 9-2. A pitcher plant (*Sarracenia purpurea*) growing in a bed of sphagnum moss (*Sphagnum sp.*).

As was mentioned above, a bog mat keeps a bog cool by acting as an insulator and a sunshade. In addition, the sphagnum moss covering the surface of a bog causes the evaporation rate to be greater than that which would occur if the depression were filled with water alone. Because, just as water evaporating from the surface of a canvas water bag cools the water inside, water evaporating from the nubbly surface of a bog mat cools the water below it. The cool temperatures that result, however, are only one of the bog's inhospitable qualities.

Take a pH reading of the water next to the pitcher plant. (Any high-school chemistry teacher should be happy to supply you with a piece of the test paper you'll need to do this, or you can order your own roll from one of the scientific supply houses listed in the Appendix.) You may have to squeeze a handful of sphagnum moss to obtain enough water. Neutral water has a pH of 7; anything below that is acid. As you'll discover, the acidity that acid rains have caused in ponds and lakes throughout the northeastern United States and Canadian provinces is simply business as usual in a bog.

Like many other forms of life, even decay bacteria find the cold, acid conditions in a bog difficult to tolerate, and this leads to another problem. In the absence of decay, nutrients are locked up in peat and the nutrient cycle breaks down. On top of that, high acidity prevents the pitcher plant from absorbing the dissolved nutrients that are present in the water. So like many a rustic unable to eke out a living on picturesque but poor soil, the pitcher plant has learned to get what it needs—particularly nitrogen—from tourists who wander in from richer areas. (Note that most of the dead insects you find inside of pitchers entered the bog as adults from other habitats.)

Boarders. All insects don't fall prey to the pitcher plant, some use it to their advantage. The *wrigglers* you noticed swimming about inside the pitchers are larvae of the tiny mosquito, *Wyeomia smithii.* They form a *symbiotic relationship* with the pitcher plant, neither helping nor harming it, as they feed on microorganisms while taking advantage of the protected habitat inside the pitchers. Wherever you find populations of *Sarracenia purpurea*, you'll find this harmless mosquito.

If you sample enough pitchers, you'll find a large (half inch to three-quarter inch) white "worm." It's a *flesh fly maggot* (*Sarcophaga sp.*), a *parasite* of pitcher plants. These maggots live in pitchers and eat insects that the pitchers capture. Antienzymes that these maggots secrete keep them from being digested along with the other insects.

Place a flesh fly maggot in a fluid-filled jar, and when it settles down see if you can discover how it obtains air. If you drop a tiny piece of raw meat in there with it, you'll find out what its two anterior hooks are for. (Note the similarities between this creep and the maggot of the goldenrod gall fly described in Chapter 7.) When the maggot is ready to pupate, it crawls out of the pitcher to complete its life cycle.

As you walk about examining pitcher plants, you'll see some small (less than an inch), sociable moths (*Exrya spp.*). As caterpillars they feed on the soft tissues inside pitchers, and in order to protect themselves while doing so, some species seal the mouths of the pitchers with silk screens; others chew rings around the necks of pitchers, which causes the tops to die, wither, and close. Still others drain pitchers by chewing holes in them; then they use the empty vessels as pupation chambers.

You can learn a great deal about a biological community by concentrating on one of its members, and that's just what you've done with the pitcher plant and the bog community. This technique works because there are no lines separating the organism from its environment. Life is a matter of relationships.

Consummating the Bog Experience

Now that you know something about bogs, you can understand why Thoreau fancied it would be a luxury to soak chin deep in one. There is a northern purity about a bog that makes immersion attractive—given a hot day, the ability to swim, and a remote bog where such an activity is ecologically prudent.

Find a spot of pure sphagnum moss where the bog mat rests on watery peat. If shifting your weight by bending your knees causes the mat to quake slightly, you're on a good spot. If the mat quakes violently, you may be on a floating section. These sections and the eye of a bog are hard to get out of without doing extensive damage to the bog mat, so try another spot. In the right place, you'll be able to go in and out without leaving a trace.

Once you've found a good spot, stand with your feet together. Then, like a nursing kitten, press with one foot then the other, rhythmically kneading the surface of the bog. You'll start to sink. When you've penetrated up to your chest, and you're sure you're in a bed of pure peat—no sticks or branches—clamber out and remove your sneakers and anything else you have on. Then ooze back in up to your chin. (When you emerge, the brown layer of peat coating your body will dry and you'll be able to brush it off.)

Relax. You're in a bog, not a swamp. There's nothing down there to nibble on your toes, so you can wiggle them with impunity. Rest your head on a pillow of sphagnum moss if you like. It's far more pure and antiseptic than the sack of chicken feathers you're used to.

After the first five minutes, you'll stop worrying about sinking out of sight. After ten minutes, you'll stop thinking about what to say if a troop of scouts enters the bog and finds your head lying there like a lost melon. And after fifteen minutes, you'll feel the breeze coming off the nearby glacier. Is it advancing or receding? No matter, there's plenty of time in a bog. When you begin to smile in response to the "dry wit of decayed cranberry vines," you're doing qualitative natural history!

LABRADOR TEA

After a boggy baptism, nothing beats a cup of Labrador tea (*Ledum groenlandicum*)—although a cup of Colombian coffee comes darn close. If you're in a bog where collecting is permitted and Labrador tea plants are plentiful, you may want to collect enough leaves for a

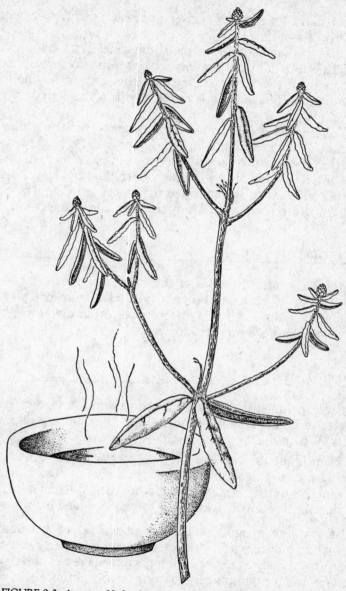

FIGURE 9-3. A sprig of Labrador tea (*Ledum groenlandicum*). Note the recurved margins and wooly undersides of the leaves.

pot. But harvest only a few leaves from each plant, so as not to cause any serious damage.

Look for Labrador tea in the shrub zone. It's a woody shrub from 1 to 3 feet tall with leathery-looking leaves on wooly stems. The margins of the leaves are *revolute* (they curl under the leaf), and the bottom of each leaf is covered with white or brown wool (Figure 9-3).

Ten leaves per cup make a strong brew, especially if they are tender, little leaves from the tops of the shrubs. Use kitchen shears to cut the leaves into very small pieces; then place them in boiling water for a few minutes and let them steep. Unused leaves can be sun dried on a screen and stored in tightly capped glass jars. Serve the tea in white bowls so you can enjoy its chartreuse color.

Conclusion

When you consider the lilies of the field, give a thought to the pitcher plant. If for lowly beetles and flies Nature has prepared voracious maggots lurking in the recesses of carnivorous plants, what might she have prepared for you?

Thought Questions

1. American Indians who lived in the eastern forests didn't have access to drugstores or supermarkets, but they did use disposable diapers. Where did they get them?

Hint: They used one of the bog plants. When dried, these plants turn into a light, fluffy material capable of absorbing eighteen times its weight in water. In addition, the dried material is so pure that until recently it was used to make padded bandages.

2. The revolute margins and wooly undersides of Labrador tea leaves retard moisture loss. Bog rosemary, another bog dweller, has similar leaves, and some species of sphagnum moss can absorb water directly from the atmosphere. How do you account for these water-saving and water-gathering adaptations in plants whose feet are constantly wet?

Hint: Plants living in a bog are like paupers living over a bank vault; they're on top of what they need, but they can't get at it. Like the pitcher plant, other bog dwellers find it difficult to use bog water because of its high acidity. Therefore, ecologists say that bogs are "physically wet, but physiologically dry" environments.

3. Certain botanists take a great interest in the pollen content of bogs. They use borers to extract samples of peat from top to bottom, and then they study the pollen in the samples. What do they learn?

Hint: Each plant species has distinctive pollen grains, and when pollen falls into a bog, it may be preserved for thousands of years in layers of peat. With the aid of these preserved pollen grains and carbon-14 dating, botanists have been able to determine the changes that have taken place in the species composition of forests over the past 12,000 years. From this they've been able to deduce the climatic changes that occurred during that period.

4. Several ways in which a bog mat contributes to the relatively low temperatures in a bog were discussed above, but there is another reason why bogs are colder than the areas around them, and this one has nothing to do with the bog mat. What is it?

Hint: Notice where the apple orchards around your home are situated. In order to avoid frosts, most apple orchards are planted on hillsides rather than on bottomland. On a local level, cold air follows certain drainage patterns. Generally it flows downhill, so it runs off hillsides and collects in low-lying depressions where it tends to persist because of the absence of disturbing winds.

5. What common plant structure was modified to produce the pitcher plant's pitchers?

Hint: Examine the fin that runs along the outside of each pitcher. You'll see that it appears to have been formed by gluing two layers together. Suppose you were to slice the pitcher open by running a razor blade right down the center of the fin, so as to separate the two layers. Then suppose you were to open and spread the pitcher flat on a table. What would it look like? (Conduct this exercise as a thought experiment only. Pitcher plants are protected in many states, and rightly so.)

Recommended Reading

GLOB, PETER VILHELM. "Lifelike Man Preserved 2000 Years in Peat." *National Geographic*, March 1954, pp. 419–430. A remarkable instance of the preservative powers of a (Danish) bog.

NIERING, WILLIAM A. *The Life of the Marsh.* New York: McGraw-Hill Book Company, 1966. Contains a well-illustrated section on bogs, and the appendix lists national parks and national wildlife refuges that include bogs and other wetlands.

SCHNELL, DONALD. *Carnivorous Plants of the United States and Canada.* Winston-Salem, North Carolina: John F. Blair, 1976. A field guide and natural history of the carnivorous plants of North America. Contains excellent color photographs, botanical descriptions, range maps, and general information, as well as a section on cultivation that includes directions for building a home bog. A beautiful and useful addition to the naturalist's library.

SLACK, ADRIAN. *Carnivorous Plants.* Cambridge, Massachusetts: The MIT Press, 1980. A general introduction to the carnivorous plant genera of the world. Good photographs and helpful line drawings. The introduction contains an interesting discussion on the evolution of pitchers.

WATTS, MAY THEILGAARD. *Reading the Landscape of America.* New York: The Macmillan Company, 1975. Chapter 5, "History Book with Flexible Covers," is about bogs. Other chapters cover habitats from the coastal dunes of Massachusetts to the terraces of the Pacific Slope in California. This is an essential book for the qualitative naturalist's library. Watts knows how to make nature signify.

CHAPTER TEN
Following the
Great Migrations

*Then the earth started to move and the Himalayas reached
for the sky. Year after year the birds [bar-headed geese]
flew their annual circuit and as the thousands of years
went by, the mountains rose beneath them. Higher and
higher they drove the geese, which in turn met the
challenge. Surely a mountain range reaching that high
through the atmosphere into the frigid lower limits of the
stratosphere would defeat the flight of birds? No—the birds
beat the mountains. Each year they accomplish the
incredible: in one majestic flight to the north in March or
April and a similar return in September or October, they
span the highest ramparts of the earth. Their flight, like a
behavioral fossil, tells of a time when the Himalayas were
small and the rivers flowed full in Tibet. The geese over
Makalu are older than the hills below them.*

Lawrence W. Swan
"Goose of the Himalayas"
Natural History, December, 1970

Two of eastern North America's most spectacular migrations are considered in this chapter: the fall migration of broad-winged hawks (*Buteo platypterus*) and the spring migration of Canada geese (*Branta canadensis*). In addition to their overwhelming beauty, these particular migrations were chosen because you won't have to travel far to see them and because the flight tactics of both migrants provide excellent opportunities to practice the delightful but dangerous art of drawing morals from nature.

The Fall Migration of Broad-Winged Hawks

William Brewster (1851–1919), the best field ornithologist of his day, characterized the broad-winged hawk as follows: "When not diverting itself with aerial flights the broad-wing is one of the most sluggish and indolent of birds, rarely undertaking any vigorous exertion which can well be avoided." "Sluggish" and "indolent" seem unnecessarily harsh, but other than that, Brewster's characterization is accurate and in a sense complimentary; for the broad-wing is truly a bird of the sky, and though it neither reaps nor sows, everything is provided for it.

FORM AND HABITS

The broad-wing is a handsome bird, somewhat smaller than a crow and easily recognized by the two conspicuous white bands on the underside of its dark tail. When seen in flight from below, its wings appear broad in proportion to its overall size, hence its common and scientific names (*platys* is the Greek word for "broad" or "flat," and *pteron* is the Greek word for "wing"). The extended wings are dark on top and light below, with blackish margins that increase in width at the tips.

Broad-wings are forest birds and do most of their hunting from perches, so you won't see them working over open fields. They're probably the hawks you've seen on dead limbs bordering small clearings along forested sections of summer highway. They also like to hunt the cleared rights-of-way under power lines that run through wooded terrain.

A perched broad-wing will let you get closer than most other hawks will allow, and when it finally takes flight, it will land nearby. If you happen to startle one, it may respond with an alarm cry that the naturalist John Burroughs called "the smoothest, most ear-piercing note in the woods."

Broad-wings nest in all of the United States east of the Mississippi and in the Canadian provinces from Alberta to New Brunswick. If you should happen upon an active nest, find a position nearby with an unobstructed view of the nest tree and the sky around it. Then sit tight and watch for the parents as they fly in with food for the young. With luck, you may see one of the archetypal images of life on planet earth: an airborne raptor clutching a writhing serpent in its talons. Granted, a broad-wing with a garter snake isn't so grand an image as the golden eagle and rattler you see on a Mexican peso, but it's a thrilling sight nonetheless and one that will burn through your retinas and brand your memory for keeps.

In addition to reptiles, broad-wings prey on large insects, amphibians, crawfish, and small mammals. These species are readily available in eastern woodlands during the summer months, but they become scarce in winter. Long before starvation becomes a problem, however, broad-wings head for Central and South America where the living is easy.

FLAPPING AND SOARING FLIGHT

True to Brewster's assertion that they don't undertake "any vigorous exertion that may well be avoided," broad-wings don't fly south under their own power; they travel as passengers in solar-powered meterological phenomena called *declivity currents* and *thermal shells*. A brief discussion of bird flight will help explain how they do it.

There are two basic forms of aerial locomotion among birds: *flapping* and *gliding* flight. Flapping flight is an energy-intensive activity in which the bird supplies all of the energy needed to overcome both gravity and air resistance, or drag, by vigorously flapping its wings. Gliding flight requires far less energy because a gliding bird sets its wings and allows gravity to overcome air resistance as it is pulled back to earth, progressing—if it is an efficient glider—as many as 15 to 20 feet forward for every foot downward.

The only problem with gliding is that in still air a bird must use flapping flight to gain altitude before each glide. But certain birds, such as hawks (including the broad-wing), vultures, and gulls, have learned to gain altitude by gliding in rising currents of air. This form of gliding, in which the bird is carried aloft by rising air, is called *static soaring.* (There is a more complex form of soaring called *dynamic soaring,* in which energy is derived from horizontal air currents, but it is employed primarily by albatrosses and other birds of the high seas, so it need not concern us here.)

DECLIVITY CURRENTS
AND THERMAL SHELLS

Broad-wings do their static soaring in *declivity currents* and *thermal shells.* Declivity currents are produced when horizontal winds are deflected upward by hills, mountains, and other obstructions (Figure 10-1). In autumn migrating broad-wings use declivity currents in situations where there are ridges running north-south and gentle to moderate winds from the north or west. Under these conditions, they tuck in their wings, close their tail feathers, and zoom along singly or in small groups like fixed-winged aircraft. Watching them flash by is exciting because they're so fast and close, but broad-wings are at their best when they're riding thermals.

Although thermals occur all year, the ones the broad-wings ride south appear on calm days in mid-September when the sun still has enough power to take your jacket off. On such days, you may see tens, hundreds, or even thousands of broad-wings in aggregations called *kettles,* tracing lazy, looping paths in the azure sky. Both the kettles and looping flight can be explained in terms of thermals.

According to an article in *Scientific American* by Clarence D. Cone, Jr. (see Recommended Reading), thermals are meteorological phenomenon that make "the energy of sunlight available to power the flight of soaring birds." Thermals begin to form as sunlight streams through the cool morning air and strikes the

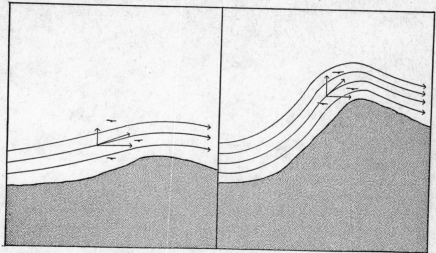

FIGURE 10-1. Declivity currents caused by hills that have deflected horizontal winds upward. Arrows indicate how the strength of the upward current is related to the velocity of wind and angle of deflection. (Based on figures by C. D. Cone, Jr. in "The Soaring Flight of Birds." *Scientific American,* April 1962.)

earth's surface. The sun's radiant heat doesn't warm the air directly, but it does warm the earth's surface, which in turn warms the air in contact with it. The air is heated unevenly, however, because the earth's surface absorbs heat at different rates depending on its color, texture, and angle to the sun; plowed fields, rock outcroppings, and parking lots, for example, warm up faster than forests and fields. On calm days, pockets of warm air form over these hot spots first, and for a while they are held in place by the layers of colder air above them. But as more heat is added, the pockets expand and rise like mushroom-shaped clouds (Figure 10-2). The cold air surrounding the base of each warm "mushroom" eventually pinches through the stem, leaving the bubble-shaped "cap" floating free as a balloon.

Each rising bubble of warm air is actually a self-contained dynamic system consisting of from several to thousands of cubic feet of circulating air. As a bubble rises through the stationary, cooler air surrounding it, fricton causes its outer layer to flow downward. This downward flow of warm air turns in on itself at the base of the bubble, rises through the center of the bubble, and again flows

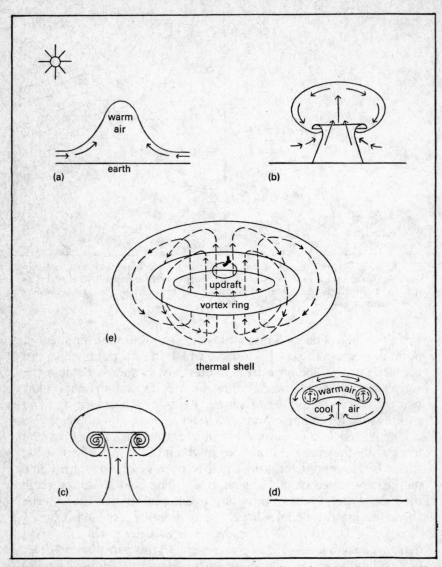

FIGURE 10-2. Development of a thermal shell. (Based on figures by C. D. Cone, Jr. in "The Soaring Flight of Birds." *Scientific American*, April 1962.)

down the bubble's outside. The entire process is repeated again and again as the bubble continues to rise. Thus, a donut-shaped mass of circulating air, or *vortex ring* (a system very much like a well-executed smoke ring), is formed. Each of these vortex rings, or thermal shells, is magnified by the masses of cooler air that are carried aloft with it.

Ever ready to take the easy way out, broad-wings ride rising thermals into the sky by gliding around inside of them. If winds are from the north, they remain inside as the thermals drift south. At such times they continue to soar in circles, but they appear to be describing long, looping paths because the thermals are moving horizontally as well as vertically.

When a thermal that is not drifting south has gained sufficient altitude, or when a thermal that has been drifting south begins to break up, the broad-wings leave it and glide downward and to the south until they encounter another rising thermal, and the process begins again. This passive, up-and-down approach is in some ways similar to traveling along a congeries of children's sliding boards with escalators for steps.

Other than the energy needed to maintain outstretched wings and to make minor steering corrections, the thrifty little broad-wings ride the cosmic rails free to Central and South America. Theirs must be a refreshing perspective as they drift leisurely along eyeing the surface of a planet where humans walk about muttering, "There's no such thing as a free lunch."

HAWK WATCHING

A day spent at an established hawk lookout is a good way to begin your hawk-watching career, although on a slow day you're apt to see more hawk watchers than hawks. You can locate the lookout nearest your home by contacting the local bird club or by checking Donald S. Heintzelman's *A Guide to Hawk Watching in North America* (see Recommended Reading). The experts you'll meet at an established lookout will help you learn to identify broad-wings and any other hawks that pass by, and they may be able to direct you to less populated lookouts.

Some of the most productive sites, such as the Hawk Mountain Sanctuary in Pennsylvania, are well known and crowded during peak periods. But broad-wings migrate along broad fronts, and even with the recent growth of recreational hawk watching, you can still find sites where you don't have to look over someone's shoulder to see the birds. In fact, in many areas clubs and organizations are looking for volunteers to gather data from isolated lookouts.

When searching for possible sites on your own, check topographic maps for geographic features such as ridges and mountains that run north-south, because broad-wings will often divert from more direct routes in order to take advantage of the declivity currents and thermals associated with these so-called *diversion lines*. Favorable weather conditions and diversion lines sometimes funnel spectacular numbers of broad-wings into a narrow corridor, producing what birders call a *grand passage*. On September 17, 1978, for example, over 11,000 broad-wings passed by the north lookout at Hawk Mountain Sanctuary as they soared south along the Kittatinny Ridge.

Broad-wings are on the move from mid-August through September. And you can expect to see the largest concentrations of them during those perfect spring days that occur in mid-September. A good day for broad-wings is often signaled by five meteorological conditions: (1) the passage of a low-pressure area over the northeastern states followed by, (2) brisk temperatures, (3) low humidity, (4) high pressure, and (5) light winds from the north or west. On days like this, climb to the lookout by nine o'clock and bring a thermos with enough hot coffee to last you until late afternoon. (You needn't arrive any earlier because thermals don't form until the sun has been out a while.)

A binocular and a field guide that shows silhouettes of hawks in flight are essential (see Recommended Reading). Broad-wings are relatively easy to identify, but in September you'll see other migrants as well, including kestrels, sharp-shinned hawks, marsh hawks, and ospreys. Some hawk watchers like to take along an owl decoy and set it on a conspicuous branch or post at the lookout. Broad-wings will ignore it, but some of the other hawks may swoop down and attack it. Warm clothing is a must, especially if you do your watching from a mountaintop. On warm days any extra clothing can be used to pad your rocky perch.

As you sit watching the proud birds glide by, it will soon become apparent to you that you're not the only one watching. Hawks are, after all, eyes with wings, and many of them will tarry a moment to get a good look at *you*. Seeing and being seen is what hawk-watching is all about. Hawks aloft!

The Spring Migration of Canada Geese

HARD-NOSING THE SKYWAYS

Canada geese are hard travelers. Unlike the easy-riding broad-wings, who soar effortlessly along the meandering paths of least resistance, geese climb into the sky under their own power and fly directly to their destinations. Moreover, while airborne they give the distinct impression that they're up there on business and that home is on the ground. No wonder we pause between our tasks twice each year and look up to them. We admire Canada geese because they remind us of ourselves.

Of course, there is more to admire about Canada geese than their dogged flight. Like the Canada goldenrod, white pine, and brook trout, the Canada goose is a North American original, and it possesses a full measure of the unexplained "smoothness" that Linnaeus first noted in North American plants, but which to varying degrees marks all of the continent's creatures. In form and habit, Canada geese exhibit the elegant but uncultivated civility that is at the heart of eastern North American wildness.

AUTUMN GEESE

You may see skeins of geese fly by in autumn while you're watching hawks, but autumn is not the best time to appreciate them because they're under intense pressure from recreational hunters. When geese come down to rest and feed during the hunting season, nothing can be trusted. Normally benign clumps of cattails harbor gunners, and flocks of their own kind (decoys) betray them. Even with careful management, *which has resulted in a steadily growing population,* mortality rates are high. Each autumn approximately one-third of the after-breeding population falls prey to hunters. Moreover, fluoroscopic (x-ray) examinations of live trapped Canada geese have shown that in some areas close to 50 percent of the adult geese have been wounded and carry one or more shotgun pellets in their flesh.

The above figures suggest why those who watch Canada geese in autumn sense something more than the usual wariness of wild birds. Canada geese are creatures not entirely unlike ourselves. They mate for life and travel in family groups. In all probability, what ethologist Konrad Lorenz (see *The Year of the Greylag Goose* under Recommended Reading) has written of the much-studied wild goose of Europe is true of the Canada goose as well:

> The family and social life of wild geese exhibits an enormous number of striking parallels with human behavior. Let no one think it is misleading anthropomorphism to say so; we have learned, systematically and thoroughly, to avoid such errors in our work. We are, however, convinced by considerations relating to the theory of knowledge that higher animals are capable of subjective experience and that they can know happiness and sadness in much the same way we do.

The geese you see in autumn are hard-pressed. Some are wounded, many have seen mates and offspring fall. Perhaps these experiences—even more than the season's dark skies and coming winter—explain the palpable sadness associated with the autumn flights.

THE SPRING FESTIVAL

Come spring and all is right between the world and Canada geese. Like groundskeepers hauling the tarpaulin from a baseball diamond, they push winter away and leave green grass behind as they follow the 30° Fahrenheit *isotherm* north. (An isotherm is a line on a weather map connecting points of equal temperature.) They're headed for the Labrador Peninsula, Akimish Island, Ungava Bay, and other breeding grounds whose very names speak of wildness and goosey splendor. The cornfields they feed in on the way are free of snow and serve up cheeselike kernels that have been mellowed in cool darkness all winter long. The geese eat heartily, honk constantly, bask in the sun, and appear to relax. Sentries notwithstanding, they'll allow you to get unusually close to them, and if you have the wisdom to obtain a seat among them, you'll feel—if not know—that the geese are celebrating what in another context the theologian Josef Pieper (*In Tune with the World.* Chicago: Franciscan Herald Press, 1965) called a *festival*:

> To celebrate a festival means: to live out, for some special occasion and in an uncommon manner, the universal assent to the world as a whole.

Spring *is* a special occasion and the geese say "Ah-onk!"

NATIONAL WILDLIFE REFUGES

Canada geese are at their best in large numbers, and in the United States you can see them that way by traveling to one of many *national wildlife refuges*, which are appropriately marked with signs bearing the image of a flying goose. In Canada, similar opportunities are available at *national wildlife areas.* There are approximately 410 national wildlife refuges in the United States, but not all of them harbor migrating geese. And of those that do, some receive their largest flights in autumn, others in spring. Therefore, it is important both to choose a refuge that attracts a large number of spring geese and to arrive there at the peak of the migration. Laura and William Riley's *Guide to the National Wildlife Refuges* (see Recommended Reading) will tell you where the geese are and their *approximate* arrival times. Addresses and telephone numbers are listed, so shortly before you leave home, you can call or write the manager of the refuge to find out what the status of the migration is. (If you do write, include a self-addressed postcard.) The timing of your visit is important because migrations vary from year to year as a result of weather conditions, and the peak spring period at a given refuge usually lasts no more than a week or two.

Although spring migrants don't tarry long, with careful planning you can still see great numbers of them in and around certain refuges. For example, the spring population of Canada geese peaks at over 100,000 during a brief period sometime in March or April at the Montezuma National Wildlife Refuge at the north end of Cayuga Lake in New York State.

An ideal day at the Cayuga festival begins with an early start from Ithaca, which is located at the south end of Cayuga Lake. Drive up the east side of the lake and have your morning coffee, such as it is, with farmers at the Triangle Diner, where plate-glass windows on three sides offer views of flatland cornfields and hundreds of feeding geese. Then motor on up the lake to the college town of Aurora, where geese can be seen and heard in the sky and on the water. Enjoy them from beneath the grove of huge sycamores, black walnuts, and cottonwoods lining the beach just before the town. There you'll learn why the ill-fated Cayugas called the spot De-a-wen-dote, place of constant dawn. Further on up the road, pull your car over to the right at the monument commemorating the destruction of the Cayuga's principal settlement by Sullivan and his troops on September 23, 1779. The hill behind the monument offers Pleistocene views of receding lake ice and mosquitolike swarms of geese swirling through the haze 10 miles and 10,000 years to the north. (The best way to get to the hill's crest is to walk up the path on the north rim of Great Gully, the stream you drove over just south of the monument.) Finally, after passing many a goose-laden cornfield, you'll arrive at Montezuma itself in time for a lurid Cayuga Basin sunset and geese tens of thousands strong.

THE VEE FORMATION

The hallmarks of geese in flight, particularly long-distance flight, are their *vee* and *echelon* (a "one-legged vee" or diagonal line) formations. If there are reasons for these formations, enough empirical studies have not been done to establish what they are. However, P. B. S. Lissamen and Carl Shollenberger (see Recommended Reading) have conducted an interesting theoretical analysis that suggests that vee and echelon formations improve aerodynamic efficiency. Theoretically, a bird flying as one of a flock of twenty-five birds in a vee formation increases its flight range by 70 percent. In other words, with an energy expenditure of x calories, a given bird can fly 10 miles on its own, or 17 miles as a member of a twenty-five-bird flock in vee formation. Again, these figures were derived from a theoretical analysis, and they may be greatly exaggerated in comparison with any advantage actually accrued during formation flight. But the fact that vee and echelon formations are used by large birds (for example, swans, geese, gulls, and ducks) on long-distance flights, where even small energy savings would be significant, lends weight to the aerodynamic efficiency hypothesis.

According to Lissamen and Shollenberger, the energy savings that birds realize when flying in vees and echelons is a result of upwelling currents of air, or _upwash fields_, that are known to occur at the tips of a bird's wings (Figure 10-3). In a vee or echelon, each goose is able to take advantage of the upwash fields from its cohorts' wings, which is tantamount to flying in a slight upward current of air. This explanation differs from the common sense explanation based on the assumption that the lead bird "pushes air aside," thus

FIGURE 10-3. Upwash currents and downwash currents created by flapping wings. (Based on a figure by P.B.S. Lissamen and Carl A. Shollenberger in "Formation Flight of Birds." _Science_, May 22, 1970.)

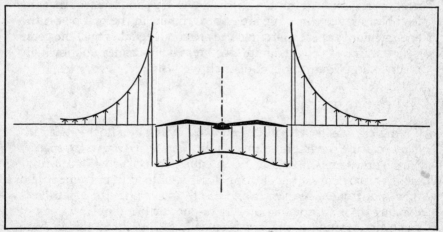

making it easier on those who follow. If the latter explanation were true, however, geese would travel in single file as do snowshoers and cross-country skiers.

Complex laws of fluid dynamics, which we need not go into here (that is, laws that I don't understand and can't explain), indicate that the total energy savings realized by a flock of geese flying in a line-abreast formation would equal the energy savings of a comparable flock flying in a vee formation. But in a line-abreast formation the energy savings would be unequally distributed, with the birds in the center realizing double the savings of the birds at either end. In a vee formation, the total energy saved is the same, but it is more equally distributed among the individual birds.

The bird in the center of a line-abreast formation saves twice as much energy as the birds on either end because it reaps the benefits of upwash fields on both sides, while the birds at the ends reap benefits on only one side. In the more equitable vee formation, the center, or lead bird had upwash fields on both sides of it, but its energy savings are less than they would be in a line-abreast formation because its cohorts are behind it, rather than directly beside it. You might expect the birds at the ends of a vee to get short-changed, just as the birds at the ends of a line-abreast formation do. But this doesn't happen because the birds at the end of a vee reap the benefits of upwash fields that have been highly developed by the birds in front of them. Given this and the fact that the lead bird's savings in a vee are not exorbitant in the first place, the energy savings of each bird in a vee are about equal. Thus, the geese whose migration flights unite two great democracies unknowingly practice an elegant form of distributive justice.

AN EXPERIENCE

To the knowledgeable observer, each landing of a flock of Canada geese can be what philosopher John Dewey (*Art As Experience.* New York: Paragon Books, 1979) called an *experience*: a self-sufficient episode consisting of distinct parts, unified in movement and flow, punctuated by pauses and rests, and moving to a satisfying conclusion or consummation. Or to put it more simply, a flock of geese landing is a short story with a definite beginning, middle, and end, in which tensions build and are finally resolved after a climax that leaves the heroes at rest.

At many refuges you can watch the landing story unfold time and again. Find a spot with a clear view of open water where geese are landing, perhaps one of the observation towers which are excellent for this purpose. If you're on one of them during a peak activity period, you'll see flocks of geese flying in the distance. Many flocks will be passing through, but occasionally one of the distant flocks will come in for a landing. After you've watched this happen several times, you'll be able to tell when a distant flock is coming in. At that moment, the story begins.

As you watch, bear in mind that geese are not cows coming home to a barn. They're wild creatures and even though it's spring-time and hunting is prohibited, they won't land without first reconnoitering the area. Moreover, flying geese are heavy birds packed with kinetic energy. If that energy is not released gradually and under full control, a sloppy landing will result, and although a sloppy landing on water might not cause any serious injuries, it would leave the birds vulnerable for a split second or two. And no wild bird will tolerate that, because in the wild sloppiness means death for some and dinner for others. A good landing leaves the geese in control of their bodies at all times, so if danger should threaten, they can maneuver past it. Goose or jumbo jet, landing is a risky business.

Before beginning the actual landing run, a large skein will make a wide pass or two over the landing site, dropping a bit in altitude with each pass. As the geese get closer to the water, the vee formation will break up into small, loose flocks called *bunches*. Pick out a bunch and stay with it.

A bunch on its final *downwind* run comes in with all wings flapping, but at some point over the landing site each goose sets its wings downward in a cowl-like configuration. Holding their positions, the geese overshoot the landing site, bank, and head *into the wind* back toward the landing site. They come in at full glide, but still high over the water and moving fast. In order to slow down, they raise the leading edges of their wings in movements functionally similar to an airplane lowering its flaps, and at the same time, they raise their heads giving their outstretched necks serpentine crooks. Not a wing beats as the geese continue to glide solemnly into the wind like a procession of robed figures with arms raised. Here the sympathetic observer senses a stillness and a concomitant building of tension comparable to that which is experienced as one's canoe enters the slick just before a Class III rapids.

Then, without warning, the set piece of gliding geese disintegrates as individuals perform spectacular flight maneuvers in which they seem to tumble about in the air. This regularity has long been noted by naturalists, and in the literature it is referred to as *sideslipping, dumping,* or *whiffling.* The first two terms, respectively, refer to airplane and parachute maneuvers that result in a rapid loss of altitude and a change in direction; however, no one has yet determined why Canada geese perform this maneuver. Two researchers (Frank H. Heppner and Christopher Willard, "Inverted Flight in Canada Geese," *Condor,* Vol. 77, No. 4, 1975, pp. 478–480) who have recorded the phenomenon on film suggest several possible reasons. One of them being:

> They might be doing it for their enjoyment. This hypothesis is not testable by present methods, but it is possible that "dumping" shares some functional characteristics with gull soaring, which may also represent a behavior which animals do, for lack of a more rigorous concept, because it feels good.

Certainly even those things an animal must do can feel good, so it is possible that there may be several reasons for the behavior. Perhaps it is a pleasurable way to decrease altitude and adjust position in a hurry. (That geese do not always whiffle when landing may be significant.)

Immediately after whiffling, the geese raise their wings high and ski in on outstretched feet. White splashes and watery vees signal the dispersal of the last of each bird's remaining kinetic energy and the consummation of the landing experience.

THE EVENING FLY-BY

Flocks of geese that have been feeding in corn fields all day start returning to the waters of the marsh in late afternoon, creating an evening fly-by that can be a grand convocation orchestrated by the setting sun. Before it begins, lie down on a grassy knoll located somewhere between the fields where the flocks have been feeding and the open, roosting waters they're heading for. If you find the right spot, skein after skein of low-flying geese will pass over as vees and echelons merge to produce an undulating filigree against the sky. When the sun is below the horizon and the white rumps of the geese are washed with evening red, put your binoculars away, forget that the patterns you're watching are composed of willful beings, and enjoy the entire display as pure sight and sound.

Thought Questions

1. It is commonly assumed that the annual southern migration of birds is triggered by shortages of food. Based on your own backyard observations, what evidence can you offer to the contrary?

Hint: Consider the robins in your backyard. Do they appear emaciated just before they leave at the end of the summer? Most birds head south well fatted and in prime condition. Lack of food may have played a role early on in the evolutionary development of migration, but a combination of external and internal factors triggers migration in most species today.

2. Broad-winged hawks travel around the Great Lakes, the Gulf of Mexico, and other large bodies of water during their migration flights. Why don't they travel directly over them?

Hint: Broad-wings depend on thermals and declivity currents. Thermals form over surfaces that absorb radiant energy at different rates, and declivity currents form when horizontal winds are deflected by trees, hills, and other obstructions.

3. Some ornithologists believe that there are more Canada geese in North America today than there were when the first European settlers arrived. What three factors, in addition to wise management, might account for this?

Hint: (1) Like cattle, Canada geese are grazers, and they readily forsake their natural diets of aquatic plants, grasses, forbs (nongrass herbs), and wild seeds for more easily obtained cultivated plants, such as corn and alfalfa. (2) Despite the influx of settlers into North America, many of the breeding areas used by Canada geese remain unspoiled because they are located in relatively un-populated regions of northern Canada. (3) During the past fifty years, numerous reservoirs have been constructed in lake-poor regions.

4. Not all Canada geese migrations involve travel between breeding areas and wintering areas. Toward the end of summer, some Canada geese leave the breeding grounds and travel *farther north*, where they remain for several weeks before beginning the fall migration south. Explain.

Hint: The migration referred to above is called a *moult migration.* As the breeding season comes to a close, Canada geese *moult,* or shed their old and tattered flight feathers. New feathers grow back within three to four weeks, but until they do the geese are unable to fly. Before the moult begins, some immature Canada geese and those who have not mated successfully fly north of the breeding grounds to areas where competition for food is less and predators are few—nice features when you can't fly. Their absence also takes some pressure off the breeding population, which also moults, but which must remain behind to care for the young.

5. Broad-wings travel mountain ridges because they are good places to find declivity currents and thermals. The origin of the declivity currents is obvious, but can you explain why thermals form on mountain slopes?

Hint: There are two reasons. One has to do with the land-slides, rockslides, and other forms of erosion that create vegetation-free surfaces on mountain slopes. The other has to do with the angles and times at which the sun's rays strike a mountainside as opposed to the flatter land surrounding it.

Recommended Reading

BELLROSE, FRANK C. *Ducks, Geese and Swans of North America.* Harrisburg, Pennsylvania: Stackpole Books, 1976. Full of current data on waterfowl, including over 20 pages on Canada geese. The population maps and migration-route maps are excellent. This book was written to replace Francis H. Kortright's classic, *The Ducks, Geese and Swans of North America*, 1942. Kortright's book lacks current data, but it makes for lively reading if you can find a copy. Both books contain T. M. Shortt's colored plates of North American waterfowl.

BENT, ARTHUR CLEVELAND. *Life Histories of North American Birds of Prey.* United States National Museum, Bulletins 167 and 170. Washington, D.C.: U.S. Government Printing Office, 1937–1938; reprint edition, New York: Dover Publications, Inc., 1958. This is one of a 23-volume set by Bent covering the birds of North America. Bent was a naturalist of the old school, and his accounts are as colorful as the birds they portray. The entire set is worth having. Bulletin 167 contains the life history of the broad-winged hawk.

————. *Life Histories of North American Wild Fowl.* United States National Museum, Bulletins 126 and 130. Washington, D.C.: U.S. Government Printing Office, 1923–1925; reprint edition, New York: Dover Publications, Inc., 1962. Bent on Canada geese and other waterfowl.

BRETT, JAMES J. and NAGY, ALEXANDER C. *Feathers in the Wind.* Kempton, Pennsylvania: Hawk Mountain Sanctuary Association, 1973. An introduction to hawk watching that will fit in your pack and serve as an excellent field guide. Photographs and silhouettes of hawks in flight are included. Available at minimal cost from the Hawk Mountain Sanctuary Association, Route 2, Kempton, Pennsylvania, 19529.

CONE, CLARENCE D., JR. "Thermal Soaring of Birds." *American Scientist,* Vol. 50, No. 1. March 1962, pp. 180–209. A brilliant analysis of soaring flight and thermal shells. For those seeking a less exhaustive, but in some ways more readable, treatment of the same subject, see Cone's article, "The Soaring Flight of Birds." *Scientific American,* Vol. 206, No. 4. April 1962, pp. 130–140.

DOHERTY, JIM. "Refuges on the Rocks." *Audubon,* July 1983, pp. 74–116. A report on the history, purposes, and current problems of the National Wildlife Refuge System.

HEINTZELMAN, DONALD S. *A Guide to Hawk Watching in North America.* University Park, Pennsylvania: Pennsylvania State University Press, 1979. An introduction to recreational hawk watching. It includes state-by-state listings of established hawk lookouts and detailed directions on how to reach them.

LISSAMEN, P. B. S. and SHOLLENBERGER, CARL A. "Formation Flight of

Birds." *Science*, Vol. 168, No. 3934. May 22, 1980, pp. 1003–1005. This paper provides an overview of formation flight and some of the theories put forward to explain it, as well as a detailed explanation of the aerodynamic efficiency hypothesis based on upwash fields.

LORENZ, KONRAD. *The Year of the Greylag Goose*. New York: Harcourt Brace Jovanovich, Inc., 1978. A book of pictures and commentary on the social life of the greylag goose, interlarded with Lorenz's comments on what it means to be a natural scientist. Although the subject is the European greylag goose, this book will enrich your experience of geese in general.

PETTINGILL, OWEN SEWELL, JR. *A Guide to Bird Finding East of the Mississippi*. New York: Oxford University Press, 1977. This book provides a brief birding survey of each state, including "precise locations of ornithological attractions and specific directions for reaching them." A good place to find outstanding hawk lookouts and prime areas for Canada geese.

RILEY, LAURA and RILEY, WILLIAM. *Guide to the National Wildlife Refuges*. Garden City, New York: Anchor Press/Doubleday, 1979. Go to this book first when you're looking for a national wildlife refuge where you can see Canada geese. It will tell you where to go, where to stay, and the best times to visit. Maps and addresses are included.

Appendix

A very *partial* list of mail-order suppliers of clothing and equipment:

Moccasins and Boots

W. C. Russell Moccasin Co.
285 S. W. Franklin
Berlin, Wisconsin 54923
(414) 361-2252

Gokeys
84 South Wabasha Street
St. Paul, Minnesota 55107
(612) 292-3911

Clothing and Gear

Eddie Bauer
Fifth & Union
P.O. Box 3700
Seattle, Washington 98124
1-800-426-6253

L. L. Bean, Inc.
Freeport, Maine 04033
(207) 865-3111

Eastern Mountain Sports, Inc.
2 Vose Farm Road
Peterborough, New Hampshire 03458
(603) 924-9212

C. C. Filson Co.
205 Maritime Building
Seattle, Washington 98104

Recreational Equipment, Inc. (REI)
P.O. Box C-88125
Seattle, Washington 98104

Fur-Felt Hats
Eddie Bauer
(see above)

J. J. Hat Center
1276 Broadway (at 33rd St.)
New York, New York 10001
(212) 239-4368

Bench Stones
Woodcraft
41 Atlantic Avenue
Box 4000
Woburn, Mass.

Binoculars
Danley's
P.O. Box 1
Fort Johnson, New York 12070
(518) 842-7853

Birding
P.O. Box 5
Amsterdam, New York 12010
(518) 842-0863

Competitive Camera Corp.
157 West 30th Street
New York, New York 10001
(212) 868-9175

Blacklights for Mothing

BioQuip Products
P.O. Box 61
Santa Monica, California 90406

American Biological Supply Co.
1330 Dillon Heights Avenue
Baltimore, Maryland 21228

Forestry Supplies

Ben Meadows Co.
3589 Broad Street
P.O. Box 80549
Atlanta (Chamblee), Georgia 30366

Forestry Suppliers, Inc.
205 West Rankin Street
P.O. Box 8397
Jackson, Mississippi 39204

Scientific Supplies

(The biology teacher at your local high school will have these catalogs on hand.)

Carolina Biological Supply Co.
Burlington, North Carolina 27215

Fisher Scientific
461 Riverside Ave.
P.O. Box 379
Medford, Massachusetts 02155
(This is the New England branch office; others are located throughout
        the United States.)

Ward's Natural Science Establishment, Inc.
P.O. Box 1712
Rochester, New York 14603

Index